It's another Quality Book from CGP

This book is for anyone doing GCSE Mathematics at Foundation Level.

It contains lots of tricky questions designed to make you sweat — because that's the only way you'll get any better.

What CGP is all about

Our sole aim here at CGP is to produce the highest quality books — carefully written, immaculately presented and dangerously close to being funny.

Then we work our socks off to get them out to you — at the cheapest possible prices.

Contents

Section Four — Statistics and Graphs

Section Five — Angles & Other Bits

Section Six — Algebra

Published by Coordination Group Publications Ltd.

Contributors:
Andy Ballard
Jane Chow
Pamela Chatley
Martin Chester
Christine Griffiths
Claire Jackson
Sharon Keeley
Simon Little
Mark Moody
Andy Park
Caroline Potter
Julie Schofield
Caroline Starkey
Emma Singleton
Sharon Watson
Jeanette Whiteman

With thanks to Vicky Daniel and Glenn Rogers for the proofreading.

ISBN-10: 1 84146 312 4
ISBN-13: 978 1 84146 312 4

Groovy website: www.cgpbooks.co.uk
Jolly bits of clipart from CorelDRAW®
Printed by Elanders Hindson Ltd, Newcastle upon Tyne

Numbers

1  Write the following numbers in order starting with the smallest:

75 61 26 57 62 16 14

....

2  Write each number in words:

(a) 579

....

(b) 6 302 457

....

(c) 26 004

....

3  Write these as numbers:

(a) twenty thousand one hundred and five

....

(b) three million four hundred thousand

....

(c) one million thirty-two thousand two hundred and thirty-seven

....

4  What does the digit 6 represent in the number 17 264?
Put a circle around the correct answer:

6 6000 600 60

Place Value

1  Without using a calculator, write down the answers to the following:

(a) $32.8 \times 10 =$ ....

(b) $328 \times 10 =$ ....

(c) $3.28 \times 100 =$ ....

(d) $46.28 \times 10 =$ ....

(e) $50.04 \times 100 =$ ....

(f) $5.4 \times 1000 =$ ....

2  An engine part weighs 23.4 grams. What would 20 identical engine parts weigh?

....

3  Answer the following questions on place value:

(a) Write down the number in the list below which is

230 230 000 23 2300 2 300 000

(i) Two thousand three hundred ....

(ii) Bigger than one million ....

(b) Write down the number "twenty-three thousand and twenty-three". ....

(c) Fill in the missing numbers in each box:

(i) $23 \times \square = 2\,300\,000$

(ii) $23\,000 \div \square = 230$

4  Put these numbers in order of size starting with the largest:

53.3 35.6 35.54 52.91 35.06

....

....

Basic Number Sequences

1 Here is a number grid:

1	2	3	4
5	6	7	8
9	10	11	12
13	14	15	16

(a) Shade in the numbers which are multiples of three.

(b) Circle the largest multiple of 5 in the grid.

(c) Which number is a multiple of 2 and also a multiple of 7?

....

2 This question is about odd and even numbers.

(a) a is odd, b is even, c is odd, d is even.

Will the following numbers be odd, even or either?

(i) $a + b$ ....

(ii) $a + c$ ....

(iii) $b + d$ ....

(iv) $a + b + 1$ ....

(v) $(a + b)^2$ ....

(b) q is an odd number. Will $2q$ be odd or even? Explain your answer.

....

....

....

(c) s is a square number. Will $s + 1$ be odd, even or either? Explain your answer.

....

....

....

Square and Cube Numbers

1 The first square number is 1.

(a) List the next five square numbers: 1 ....

(b) Which of your five numbers are odd?

....

2 Write down all the square numbers between 40 and 70.

....

3 Which cube numbers are between 100 and 400?

....

4 Stephanie is thinking of a number between 10 and 30.

(a) It is an odd number which is also a square number. What number is Stephanie thinking of?

....

(b) Simon is thinking of a 2-digit square number. He realises that it is also a cube number. What number is Simon thinking of?

....

5 This question is about square and cube numbers.

(a) What is the difference between the second and third square numbers?

....

(b) James is thinking of two consecutive square numbers less than 100. The difference between them is also a square number. What two numbers could James be thinking of?

....

....

(c) Fran is thinking of two square numbers less than 100. The difference between these is a cube number. What two numbers could Fran be thinking of?

....

....

Factors

1 This question is about the factors of 24.

(a) List all the factors of 24.

....

(b) Which factors of 24 are also cube numbers?

....

(c) Which factors of 24 are also square numbers?

....

2 What is the total of all the factors of 20?

....

3  Complete the following table:

Number	Factors
10	1, 2, 5, 10
12	
14	
16	

4  Here is a number grid:

1	2	3	4	5	6
7	8	9	10	11	12
13	14	15	16	17	18
19	20	21	22	23	24
25	26	27	28	29	30

(a) Put a circle around all the numbers which are multiples of 5.
One of them has been done for you.

(b) Put a square around all the factors of 36. One of them has been done for you.

Ratios

1 Divide £180 in the ratio 7:2.

....

....

2 £55,000 of lottery money is to be shared between two local cricket clubs in the ratio 3:2.
How much money will each club receive?

....

....

3 There are 18 girls and 12 boys in a maths class.
Write this as a ratio of girls to boys in its simplest form.

....

....

4 Boxes of eggs are sold in a farm shop. Six boxes cost £3.30.
How much would eight boxes cost?

....

....

5 The diagram is made up of 20 square tiles. Some are grey. The others are white.

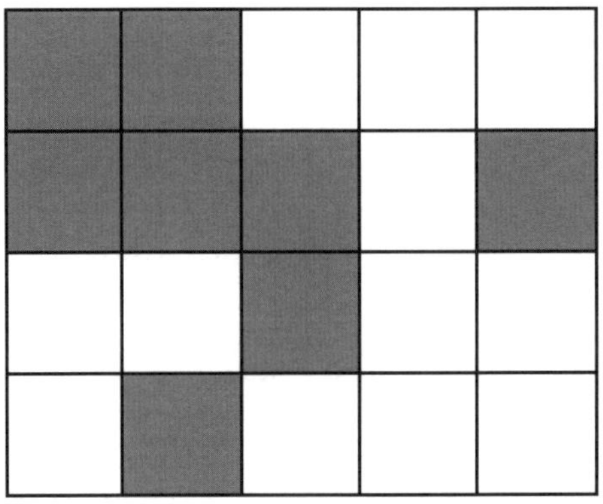

What is the ratio of white tiles to grey tiles in its simplest form?

....

....

Ratios

1 David is shopping for oranges. He can buy a bag of seven oranges for £1.40 or single oranges for 24p each. Which is better value for money? Explain your answer.

....

....

....

2 A new dog food comes in cans of two different sizes.
The small can is 300 g and costs 50p, while the large can is 500 g and costs 80p.
Which size can is better value for money?

....

....

....

3 Brown sauce can be bought in three different sizes. The price of each is shown below.
Which size of bottle is the best value for money?

125 ml £1.15 | 250 ml £2.30 | 500 ml £4.10

....

....

....

4 William wants to buy some wallpaper.
The paper he likes comes in rolls of two different lengths.
Ten-metre rolls cost £3.49. Six-metre rolls cost £2.10.
Which length of roll should William buy to get the best value for money?

....

....

....

Using Formulas

1  Work out:

(a) $5 + 2 \times 3 =$ ....

(b) $10 + 4 \div 2 =$ ....

(c) $4 \times 2 - 2 =$ ....

2  If $x = 5$ and $y = 4$, work out:

(a) $6x + y$

....

(b) $x^2 - y^2$

....

(c) $y^3 - x^2$

....

3 Insert brackets to make these equations true:

(a) $56 \div 4 + 3 = 8$

(b) $5 + 2 \times 3 + 6 = 63$

4 Work out:

(a) $6 + \frac{10}{2} =$ ....

(b) $\frac{6 + 10}{2} =$ ....

5 If $s = 8$ and $t = 2$, work out:

(a) $(s + t)^2$

....

(b) $2(s - t)$

....

Numbers Mostly Mini-Exam (1)

1 The total number of supporters at a hockey match is 13 692.

(a) Write down the number 13 692 in words.

....

(b) In the number 13 692 write down the value of:

(i) the figure 6

....

(ii) the figure 3

....

2 Read this list of numbers:

5 6 9 10 12 14 28 32 49

From the list write down:

(a) a multiple of 8

....

(b) two square numbers

....

(c) two factors of 28

....

3 Work out the answers to these:

(a) Find the value of $4q - 3p$ when $q = 2$ and $p = 1$.

....

....

(b) Find the value of $x^3 - y^2$ when $x = 4$ and $y = 3$.

....

....

Numbers Mostly Mini-Exam (1)

4 This question is about odd and even numbers.

(a) n is an even number.
Will $3n - 1$ be an "even number", an "odd number" or "either odd or even, depending on the value of n"? Tick the correct box:

EVEN NUMBER ☐ ODD NUMBER ☐ EITHER ODD OR EVEN ☐

(b) p is an odd number.
Will $2p + 4$ be an "even number", an "odd number" or "either odd or even, depending on the value of p"? Tick the correct box:

EVEN NUMBER ☐ ODD NUMBER ☐ EITHER ODD OR EVEN ☐

(c) m is a whole number. m^3 could be an odd number or an even number. Explain why.

....

....

....

5 The cost in pounds of hiring a cement mixer is found using the following formula:

$$\text{Cost} = (12 \times \text{number of days hired}) + 10$$

Calculate the cost of hiring a cement mixer for:

(a) three days

....

....

(b) one week

....

....

Numbers Mostly Mini-Exam (2)

1 Here is a set of numbers:

10 16 21 23 28 36

(a) Which of these numbers is a multiple of both 4 and 7?

....

(b) Write down two of these numbers that have a difference of 7.

....

(c) Which two numbers are square numbers?

....

2 There are 8760 hours in a normal year.

(a) What value does the figure 7 represent?

....

There are 60 minutes in an hour.

(b) How many minutes are there in a normal year?

....

....

(c) Write your answer to part (b) in words.

....

....

Numbers Mostly Mini-Exam (2)

3 Jayne has received a bonus from work of £81.25 and wants to share it with her brother Karl. She decides to divide the money in the ratio of their ages. Jayne is 16 years old and Karl is 9 years old. How much money will Karl receive?

4 If $a = 13.2$ and $b = 5.6$, work out:

(a) $a^2 + b$

(b) $3a - b$

(c) $b^3 - a^2$

5 Sports socks are sold in packs. A pack of three pairs costs £2.50. A pack of ten pairs costs £7.10. Which pack is better value?

Perimeters

1 Find the perimeter of the rectangle below.

5 cm

3 cm

Not to scale

....

....

2 Calculate the perimeters of each of the shapes below. (Diagrams not to scale.)

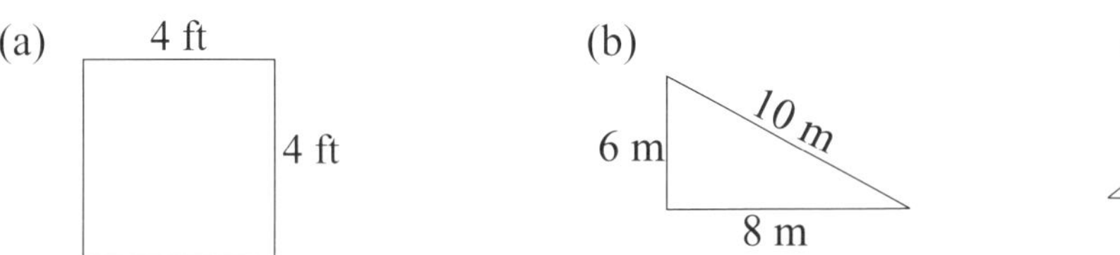

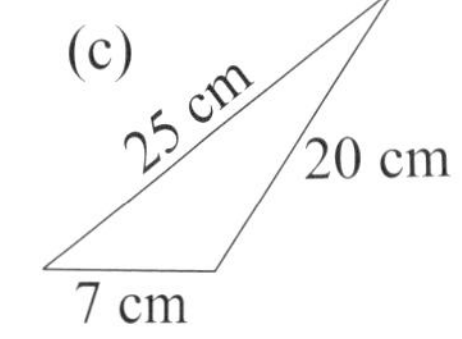

(a) ....

(b) ....

(c) ....

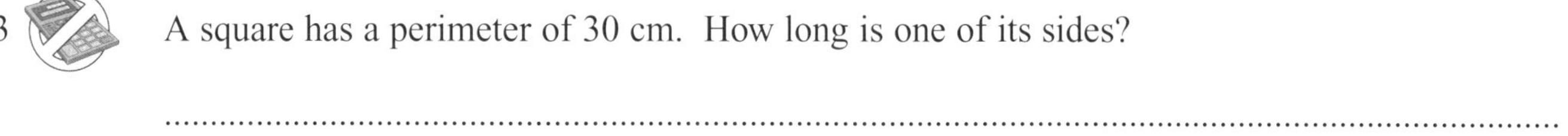

3 A square has a perimeter of 30 cm. How long is one of its sides?

....

....

4  An equilateral triangle has a perimeter of 12 m. How long is each side?

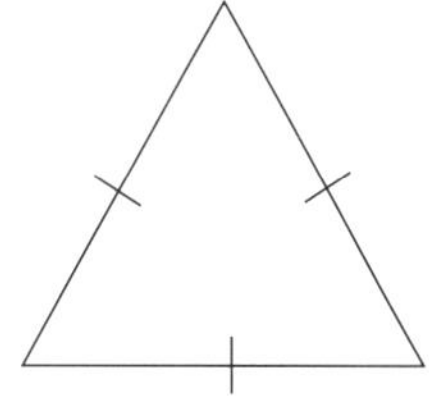

Not to scale

....

....

Circumference

1 Calculate the circumference of each circle.

(a)

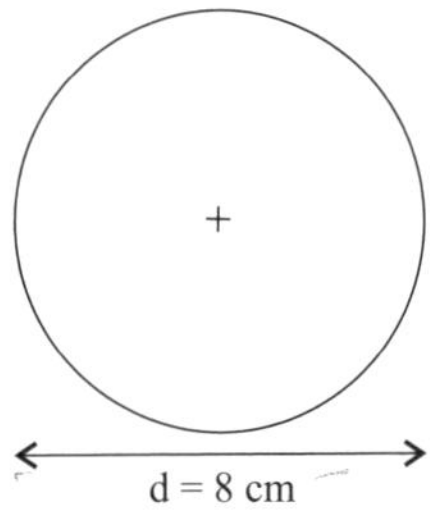

Diagrams not to scale

(b)

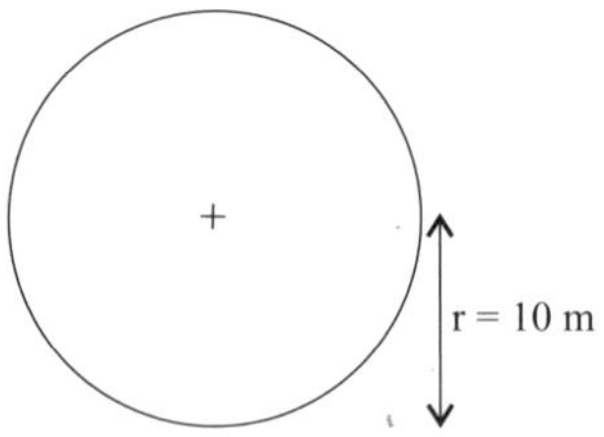

(a) ....

(b) ....

2 Find the perimeters of each of the shapes below.

(a)

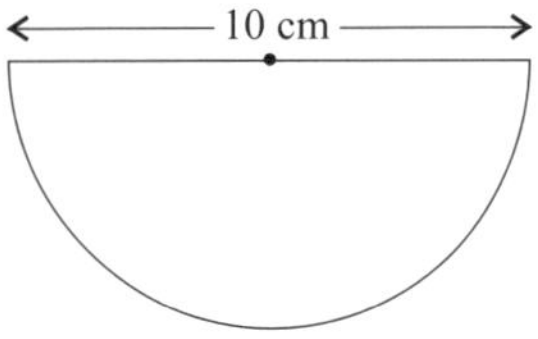

Not to scale

(b)

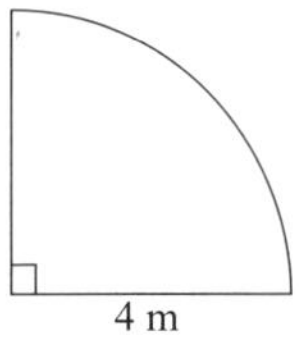

(a) ....

(b) ....

3 A bicycle wheel has a diameter of 700 mm. The wheel goes round 120 times as the cyclist rides to a friend's house. How far does the cyclist travel (to the nearest metre)?

....

Areas

1  Find the area of each shape:

(a)

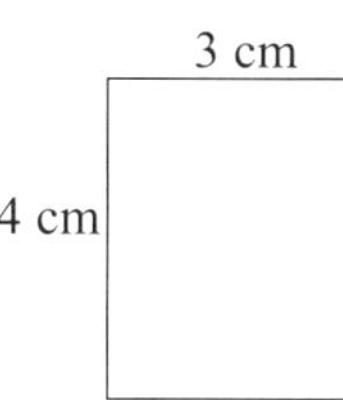

(b)

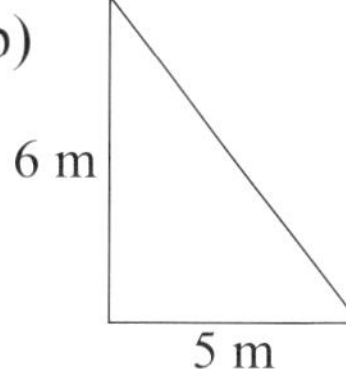

(c)

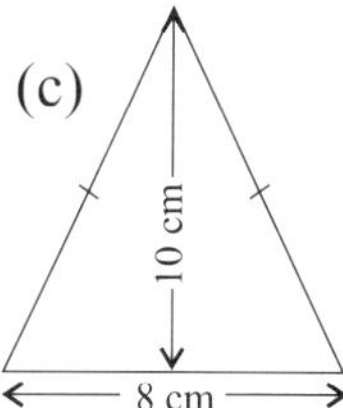

Not to scale

(a) ....

....

(b) ....

....

(c) ....

....

2 Find the area of the room below.

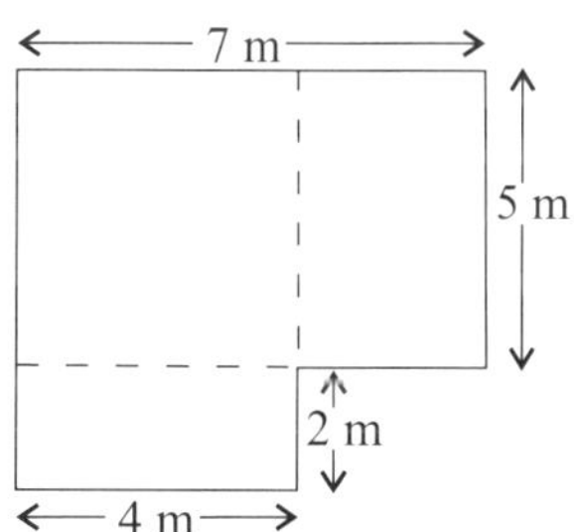

Not to scale

....

....

....

3  A Christmas decoration is made of card using a square and four isosceles triangles as shown on the right. Find the total area of card used.

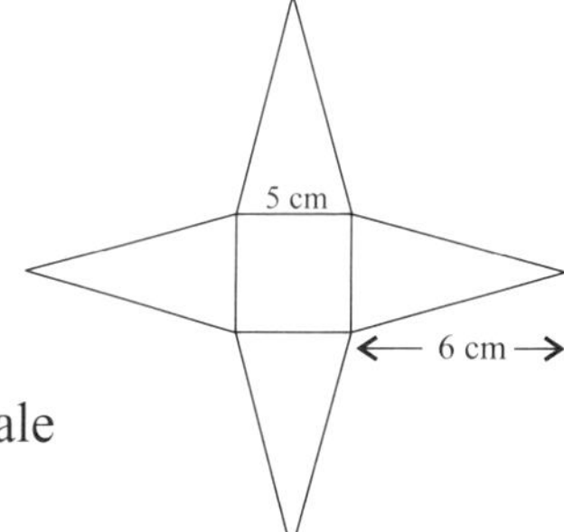

Not to scale

....

....

....

Areas

1 Calculate the area of each circle shown below:

(a)

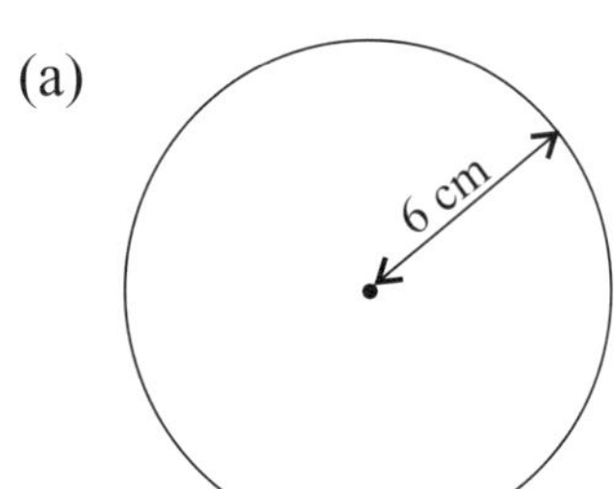

(b)

14 m

Not to scale

(a) ....

....

(b) ....

....

2 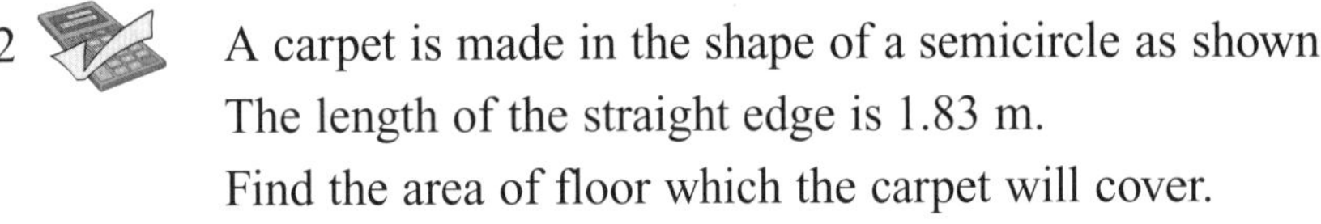

A carpet is made in the shape of a semicircle as shown.
The length of the straight edge is 1.83 m.
Find the area of floor which the carpet will cover.

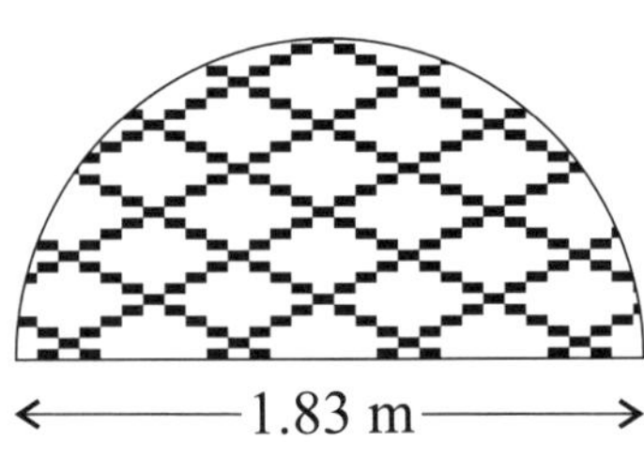

....

....

....

3  A flower bed is in the shape of three identical quarter circles joined together as shown.
Each quarter circle has a radius of 2 m. Find the area of the flower bed.

....

....

....

....

....

Solids and Nets

1  The diagram shows a cuboid.

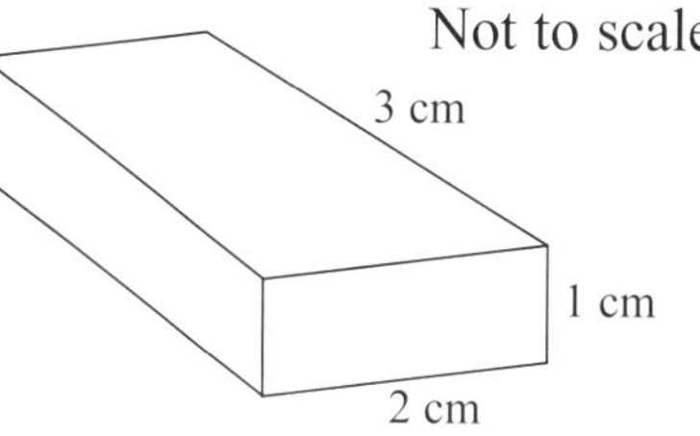

(a) In the space below **sketch** a possible net for the cuboid.

(b) How many faces, edges and vertices does the cuboid have?

Faces = ... Edges = ... Vertices = ...

2  A square-based pyramid is shown below. Draw an **accurate** net of the pyramid.

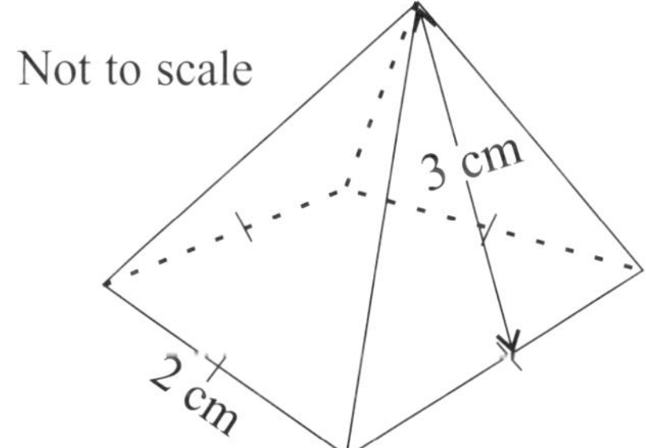

3  The diagram shows a hollow paper cone with a circular paper base.
Sketch a net of the paper shape in the space below.

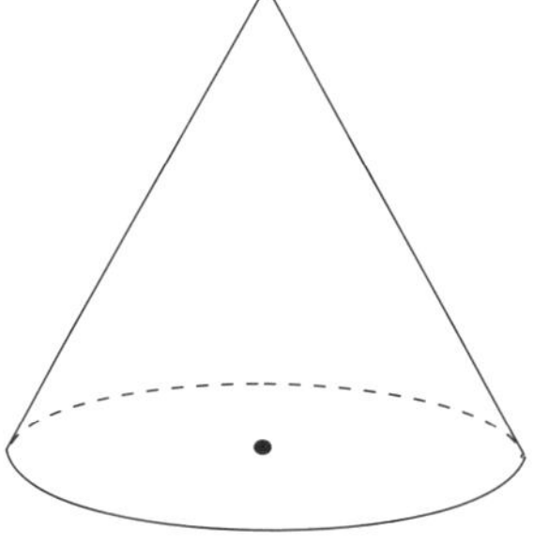

Projections

1  A diagram of a house is shown:

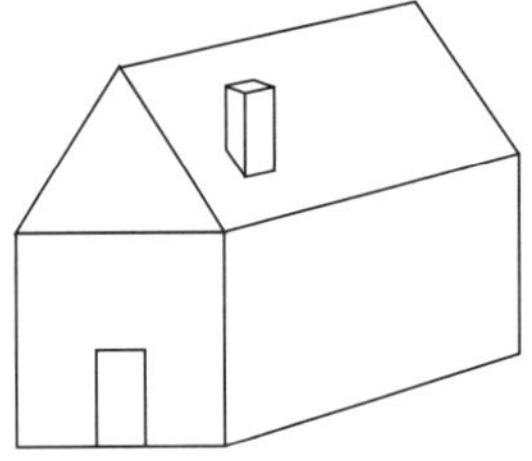

(a) Draw a sketch of the plan view of the house.

(b) Draw a sketch of the side view of the house as seen from B.

2  A three-dimensional solid made from 20 cubes is shown in the diagram:

(a) Draw the side elevation as seen from X.

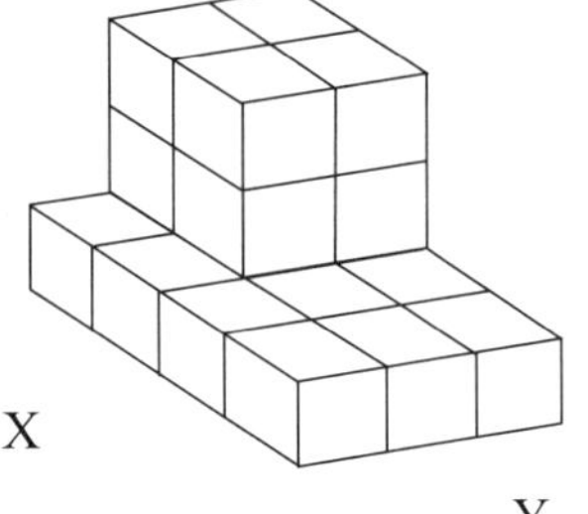

(b) Draw the front elevation as seen from Y.

Volume

1  The sides of a cube-shaped cardboard box are all 4 cm long.

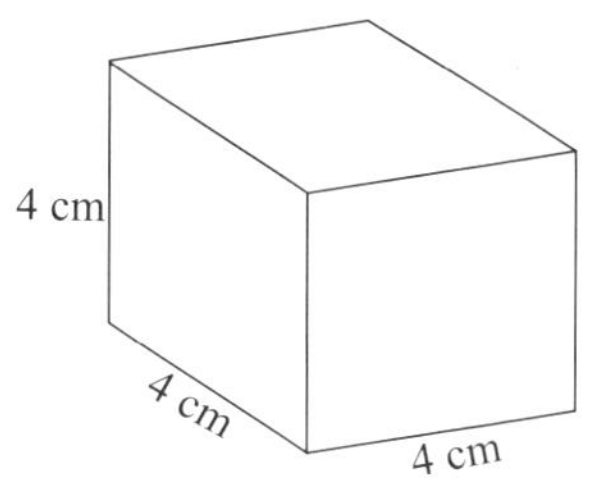

Not to scale

Find the volume of the box.

....

....

....

2 The diagram shows an open-topped cardboard box in the shape of a cuboid.

14 cm
6 cm
10 cm

Not to scale

(a) Calculate the volume of the box.

....

....

(b) How many cubes 2 cm by 2 cm by 2 cm would fit inside the box?

....

....

3 A container has a volume of 18 m^3. Its dimensions are 2 m by 3 m by 3 m.
A different sized container also has a volume of 18 m^3. What could its dimensions be?

……….. m by ………… m by ………….. m

Symmetry

1  Shade in four squares in the grid below so that line AB is a line of symmetry.

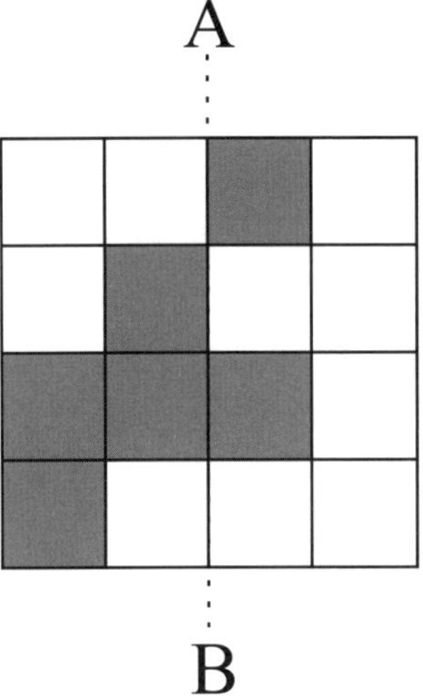

2 Reflect the triangle in the mirror line.

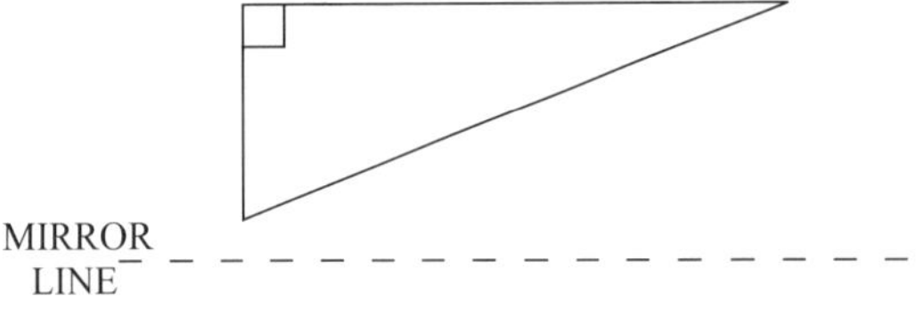

3 Draw a plane of symmetry on each shape.

(a) Cuboid

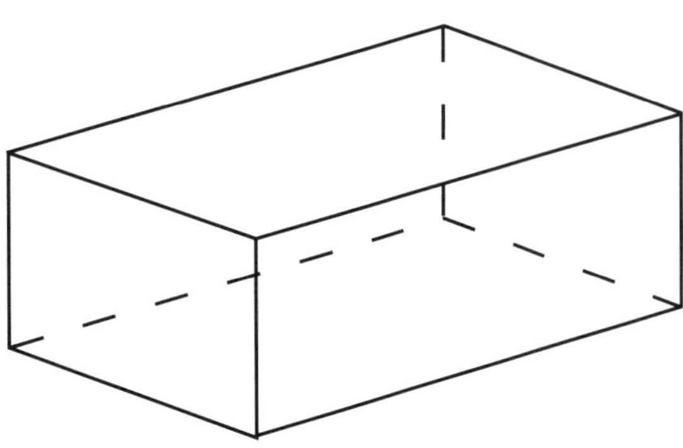

(b) Cube

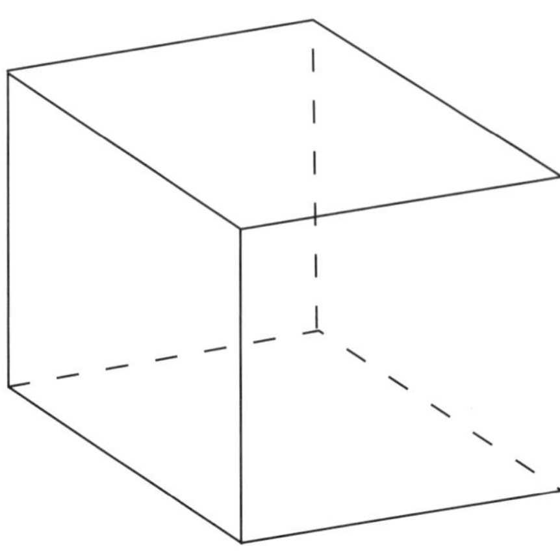

Symmetry

1  What is the order of rotational symmetry for each shape?

(a) 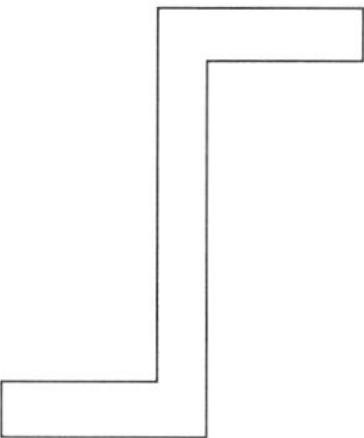

Order = ...

(b) 

Order = ...

(c) 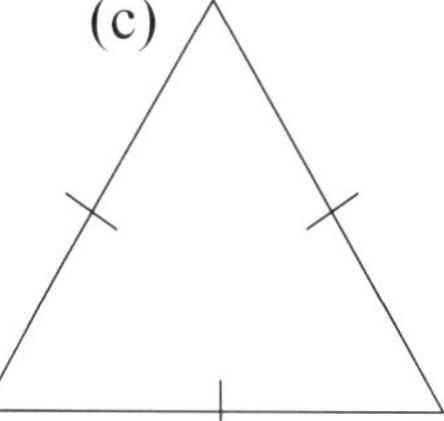

Order = ...

2  Continue this tessellation by adding at least four shapes:

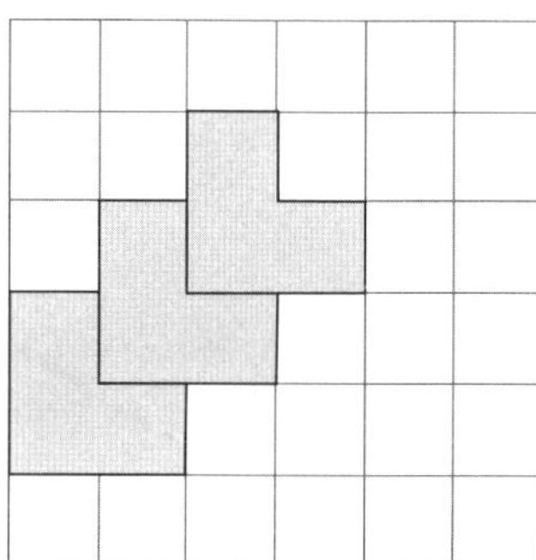

3 This diagram shows five pentominoes. Each one is made with five small squares.

A 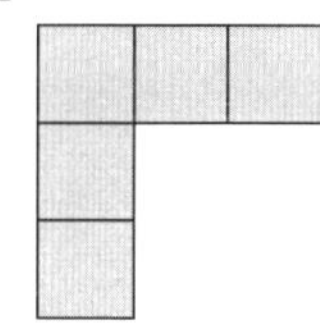

B 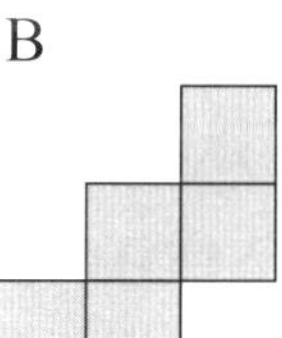

C 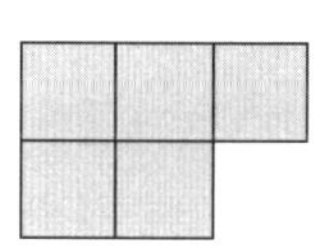

D 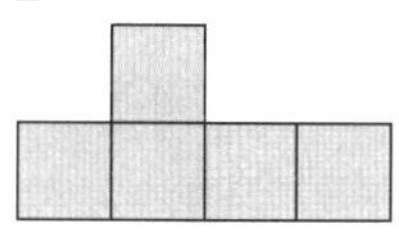

E 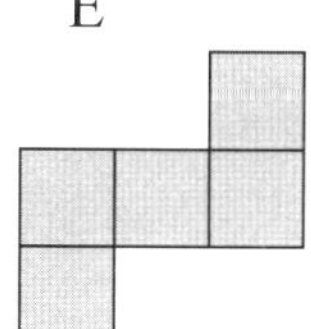

Which pentominoes have:

(a) one line of symmetry? ....

(b) rotational symmetry of order 2? ....

Shape D is redrawn below.

(c) Add one more square to the diagram so that shape D has rotational symmetry of order 2.

The Shapes You Need to Know

1  Name each of the following shapes:

(a) 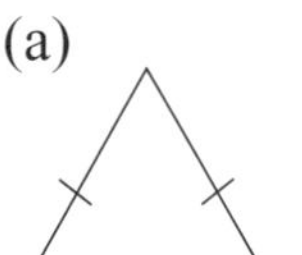 (b) (c) 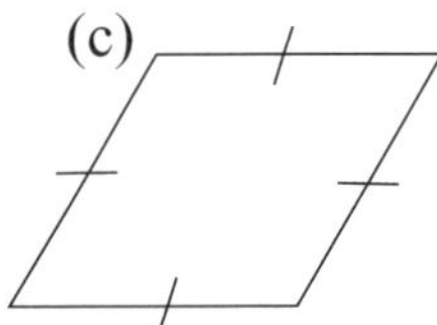 (d) 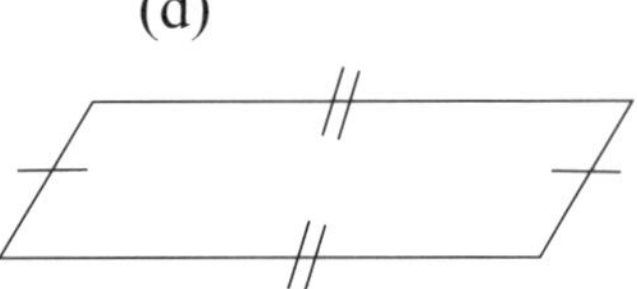

(a) .... (b) ....

(c) .... (d) ....

2  Match each solid to its name. One has been done for you.

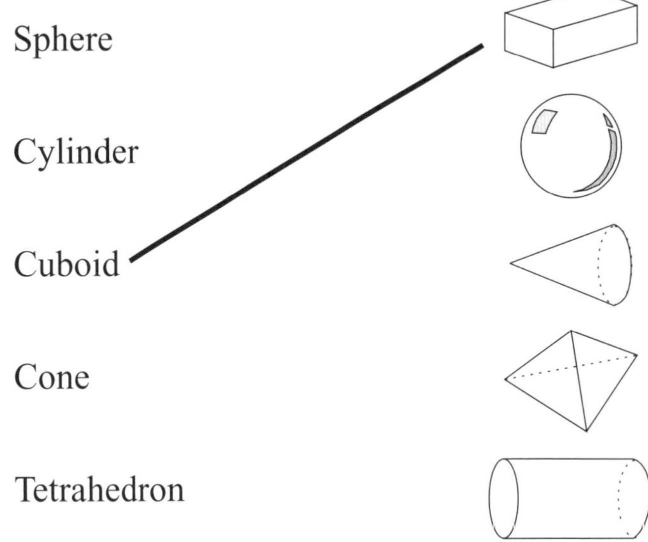

3  Sketch a regular pentagon below.

4  How many sides do the following shapes have?

(a) Hexagon ....

(b) Heptagon ....

Regular Polygons

1 The diagram shows a regular polygon.

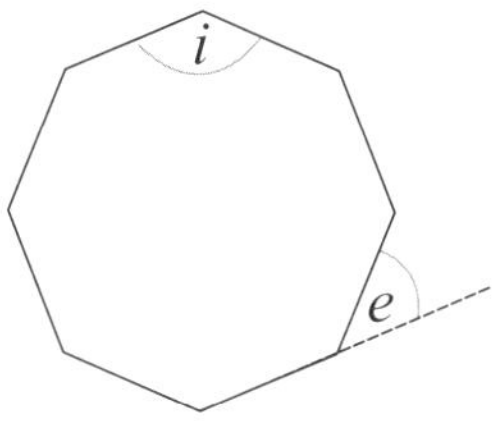

(a) Write down the mathematical name of the polygon.

....

(b) Work out the size of the exterior angle marked e.

....

....

(c) Work out the size of the interior angle marked i.

....

....

2 A football is made up of regular pentagons and regular hexagons.

A sector triangle AOB has been drawn in the pentagon.

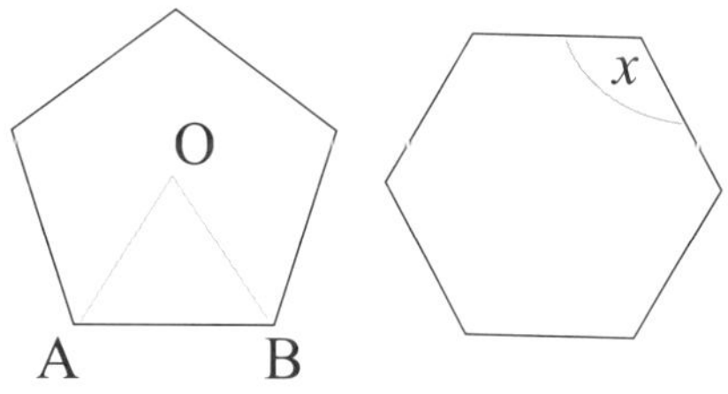

(a) Triangle AOB is a special type of triangle. Write down its mathematical name.

....

(b) Draw lines in the pentagon to show four more sector triangles.

....

(c) Work out the size of angle AOB.

....

....

(d) Work out the size of angle x in the hexagon.

....

....

Regular Polygons

1 A tile ABCED is made from a square ABCD attached to an equilateral triangle CDE.

Their common side is CD.

Not to scale

(a) Work out the size of angle y.

....

....

(b) Work out the size of the interior angle ADE.

....

....

2 A 50p piece is in the shape of a regular polygon (though with rounded corners).

(a) What is the mathematical name for the shape of the polygon of a 50p piece?

....

(b) Calculate the exterior angle of a 50p piece. Give your answer to 2 decimal places.

....

....

(c) Calculate the sum of the interior angles of a 50p piece.

....

....

3 A decagon is a polygon with 10 sides.

Work out the difference between the sizes of an interior angle and an exterior angle of a regular decagon.

....

....

Shapes Mini-Exam (1)

1  Paul buys some unusually shaped floor tiles.

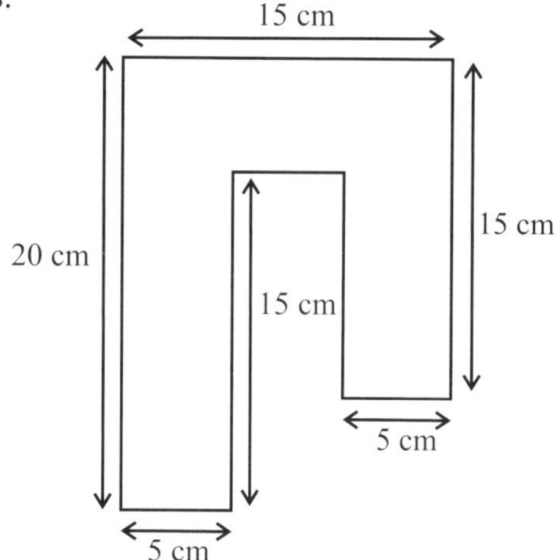

(a) Work out the perimeter of the tile.

....

....

(b) Paul places a tile on the floor.

He is unsure of how to lay the remaining tiles.

Using the grid on the right, draw another 7 tiles to show how they tessellate.

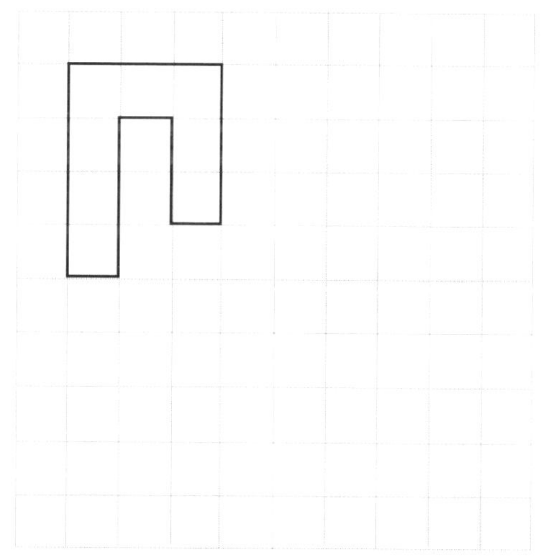

(c) Reflect the tile in the line AB.

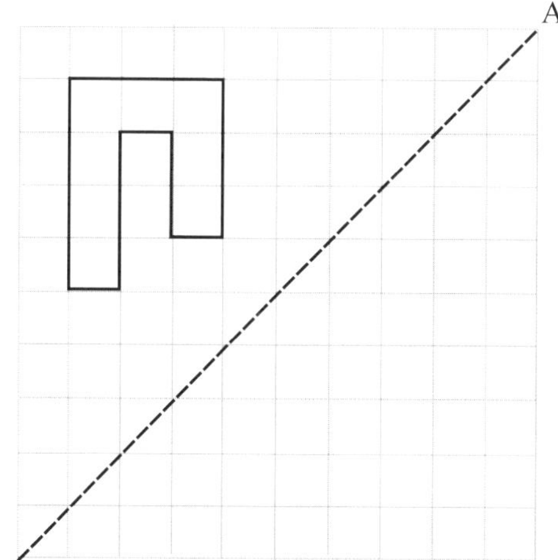

Shapes Mini-Exam (1)

2  Here is the net of a solid made from a square with identical triangles attached to each side.

The length of each side of the square is 5 cm.

The height of each triangle is 12 cm.

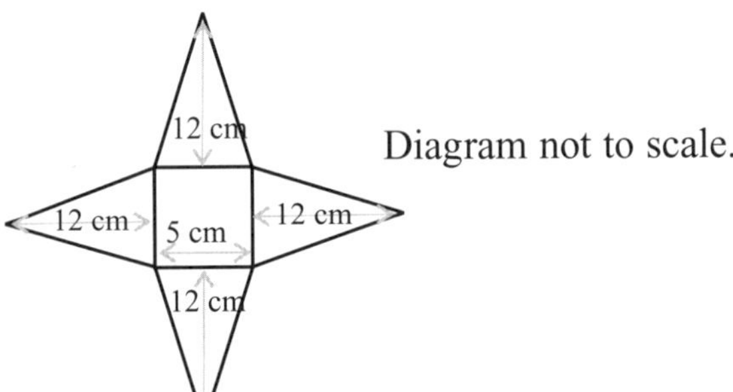

(a) Write down the name of the solid formed from the net.

....

(b) Write down the number of lines of symmetry of the net.

....

(c) Work out the area of the net.

....

....

3 There are different kinds of symmetry.

(a) Complete this pattern so it has rotational symmetry of order 4.

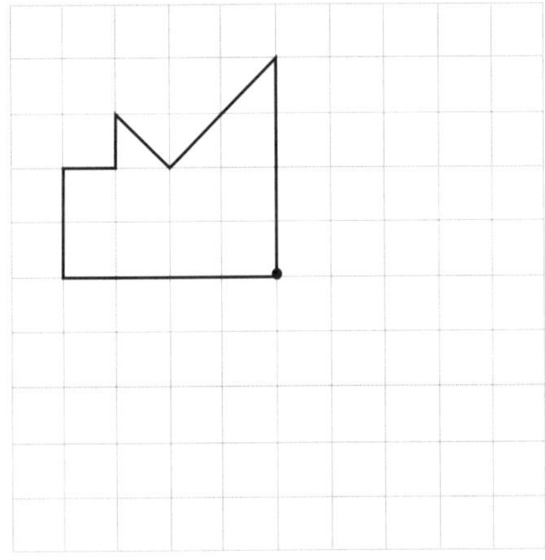

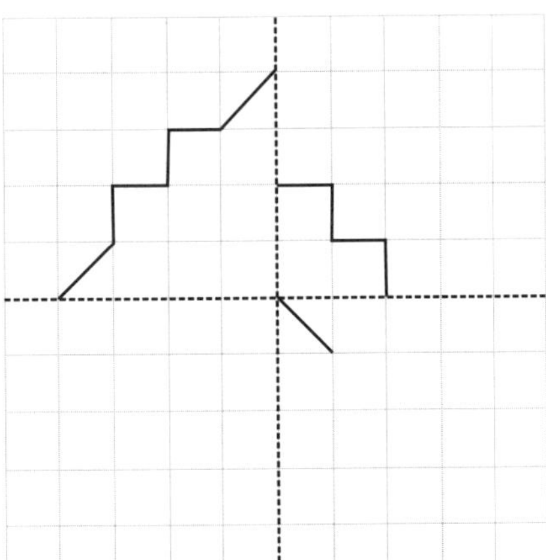

(b) The diagram shows part of a badge.

The dotted lines are lines of symmetry of the badge.

Complete the badge.

Shapes Mini-Exam (2)

1  The diagram shows six chocolate biscuits on a rectangular tray.

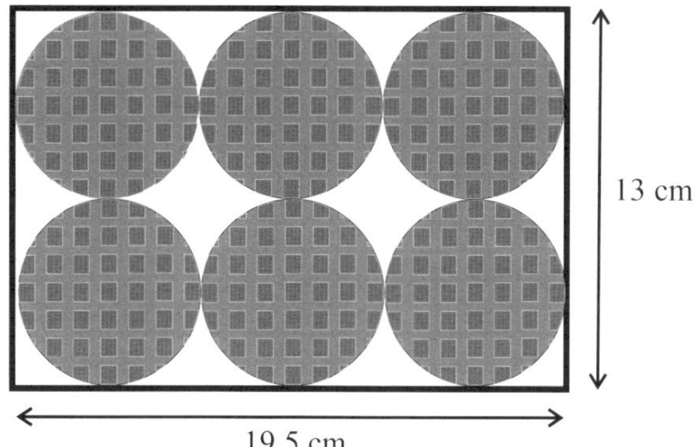

(a) Work out the area of the tray.

....

....

(b) Work out the area of one chocolate biscuit.
Assume the biscuits take up the full width and length of the tray, as shown.
Give your answer to 1 decimal place. Use the value of π on your calculator.

2  A goldfish tank of length 90 cm and width 30 cm is filled with water to a depth of 40 cm.

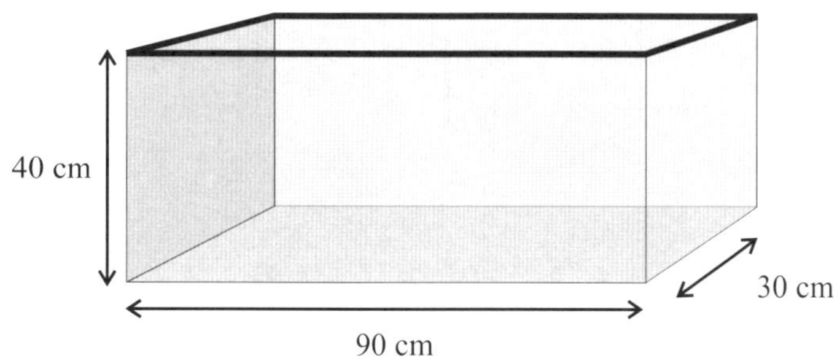

(a) Calculate the volume of water in the tank.

....

(b) To avoid overcrowding in the tank, each goldfish needs 6000 cm^3 of water.
Work out the greatest number of goldfish the tank will hold.

....

Shapes Mini-Exam (2)

3  The radius of David's bicycle wheel is 0.25 m.

(a) Calculate the circumference of the wheel.
Use $\pi = 3.14$ in this calculation.

....

....

(b) David's school is 500 m from his house.

Calculate how many complete turns the bicycle wheel makes when David rides to school from home.

....

....

4  The picture shows a section of honeycomb.
The honeycomb is made from regular hexagons.
The length of the side of each hexagon is 3.85 mm.

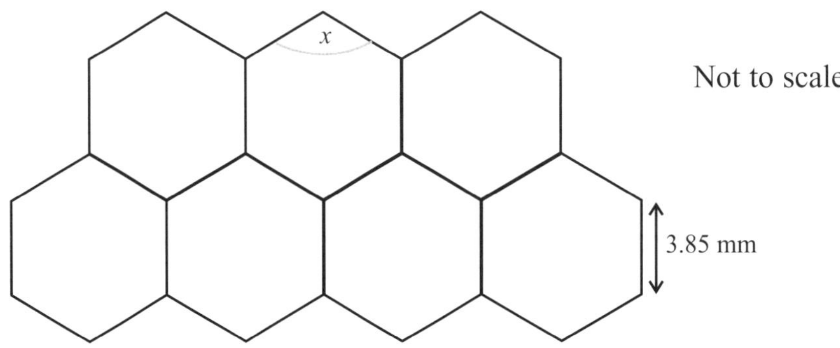

(a) Work out the perimeter of the section of honeycomb shown.

....

....

(b) Work out the size of angle x.

....

....

Converting Units

1 This question is all about conversion factors.

(a) The length of a classroom is 746 cm. How long is that in metres?

....

(b) A bunch of bananas weighs 1.3 kg. How much is this in grams?

....

(c) A large container of orange juice contains 2.5 litres. How much is that in millilitres (ml)?

....

2 The diagram below shows the plan of a classroom. The teacher's desk is shown in grey.

(a) Approximately how long and how wide is the classroom in yards?

(i) Width = ...

(ii) Length = ...

class length = 746 cm

class width = 580 cm

desk length = 56 in

desk width = 24 in

(b) How long is the teacher's desk in feet and inches?

....

(c) Approximately how wide is the teacher's desk in centimetres?

....

3 Weights are often given in metric units (e.g. grams and kilograms) or imperial units (e.g. stones, pounds and ounces).

(a) Approximately how much does an 8 kg sack of potatoes weigh in pounds (lb)?

....

(b) How many grams does a 3.6 kg box of apples weigh?

....

(c) Annabel weighs 10 stone 4 pounds.

(i) How many pounds is this?

....

(ii) What is her weight in kg (approximately)?

....

Rounding Off

1 Ted has three pencils of different lengths.

(a) Pencil A is 15.4 cm long. What is this to the nearest centimetre?

....

(b) Pencil B is 13.78 cm long. What is this to the nearest 0.1 cm?

....

(c) Pencil C is exactly halfway between 14.2 cm and 14.3 cm.
How long is pencil C to the nearest 0.1 cm?

....

2 Maggie wanted to send three parcels to different parts of the UK, so she went to the post office and picked up the leaflet below about postage.

Weight up to	First Class	Second Class
60 g	28p	20p
100 g	42p	34p
150 g	60p	46p
200 g	75p	56p
250 g	88p	69p
300 g	£1.01	80p
350 g	£1.15	91p
400 g	£1.37	£1.10
450 g	£1.56	£1.25
500 g	£1.74	£1.42
550 g	£2.10	£1.68

(a) Uncle Tom's gift weighed 530 g. His birthday was next day so Maggie decided to send it first class. How much did it cost to send?

....

(b) Alice's parcel weighed 255 g. How much did Maggie pay if she sent it second class?

....

(c) Maggie sent her daughter's package first class. The parcel weighed 490 g. How much did Maggie pay to send it?

....

3 It can be very useful to round figures to a certain degree of accuracy.

(a) The attendance at a football match was 2568 people. What is this to the nearest hundred?

....

(b) The distance from Barnham to Farnchester is 26.38 miles. What is this to the nearest mile?

....

(c) An oil tank contains 7.84 litres of oil. How much is this to the nearest 0.1 litre?

....

Rounding Off

1 Measurements are sometimes rounded to a certain number of decimal places.

(a) (i) The area of a circle is 21.73 cm^2. What is this to 1 decimal place?

(ii) The circumference of the same circle is 16.525 cm. Round this off to 2 decimal places.

(b) (i) A triangle's base measures 12.27 m. What is this to 1 decimal place?

(ii) The area of the same triangle was found using a calculator.
The calculator read 59.1414 m^2. What is this to 2 decimal places?

2 The table shows the heights of the highest mountains in Scotland, Wales and England.

Mountain	Height (metres)
Ben Nevis	1344
Snowdon	1086
Scafell Pike	979

(a) How high is Ben Nevis to the nearest thousand metres?

(b) How high is Snowdon to the nearest hundred metres?

(c) Round the height of Scafell Pike to:

(i) the nearest hundred metres.

(ii) the nearest ten metres.

3  Round these numbers to the stated number of significant figures:

(a) to 1 significant figure:

(i) 84 (ii) 3.6 (iii) 270

(b) to 2 significant figures:

(i) 229 (ii) 4.65 (iii) 76.2

(c) to 3 significant figures:

(i) 2346 (ii) 142.6 (iii) 8307

Estimating and Approximating

1 Find approximate answers for the following:

(a) 24.8×9.6 ....

(b) $228 \div 18.6$ ....

(c) $\dfrac{658 + 214}{316}$ ....

(d) $\dfrac{16.8}{3.7 + 2.4}$ ....

2  The formula for the volume of a cylinder is $V = \pi \times r^2 \times h$.
Estimate the volume of the cylinder on the right.
(Use a suitable estimate of $\pi = 3.14159...$)

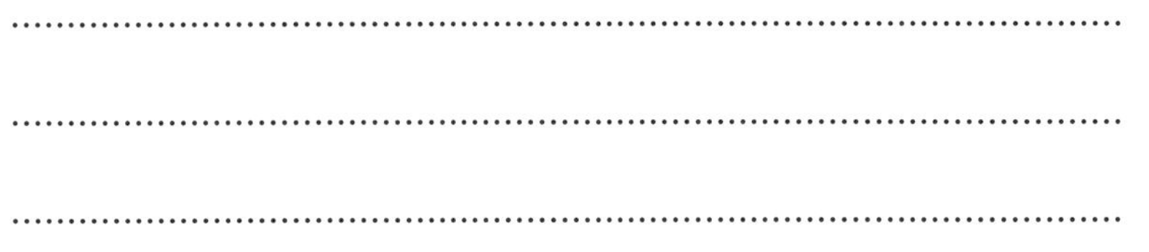

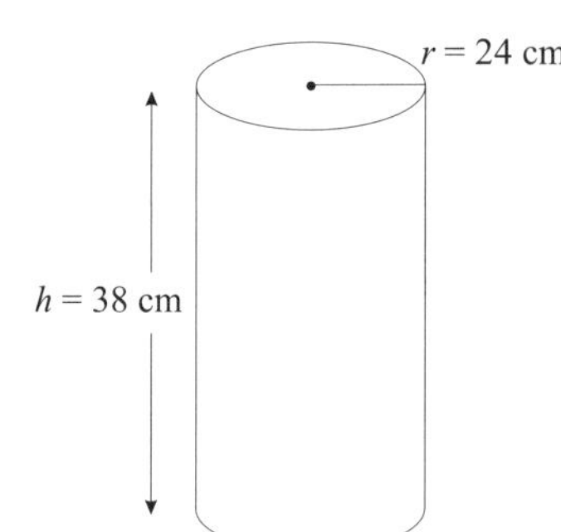

3  Look at the map of Sri Lanka. Estimate the approximate area of Sri Lanka.

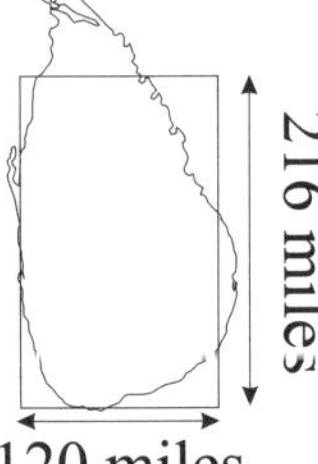

....

4  A piece of card measures 28 cm by 63 cm. What is its approximate area?

....

5 Estimate the approximate volumes of the sauce bottles shown.

(a) Bottle A: ....

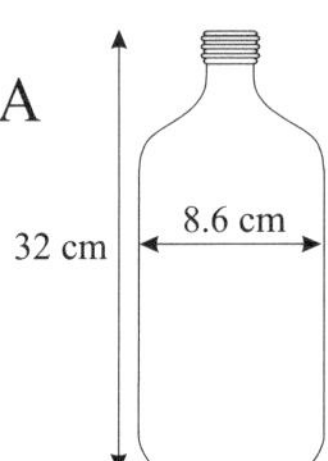

(b) Bottle B: ....

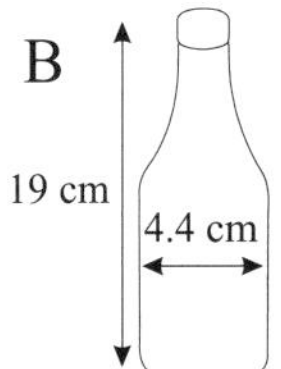

Conversion Graphs

1  The Campbells are going to Canada on holiday. Each member of the family takes their own spending money. Use the graph below to answer the following questions.

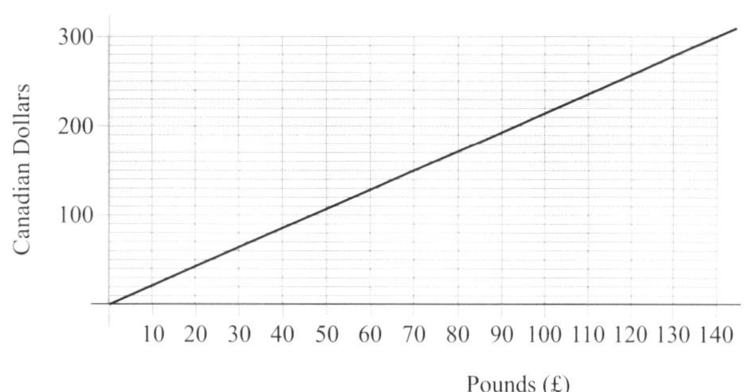

(a) Mary takes £120. Roughly how much is this in Canadian dollars? ....

(b) Convert Robert's pocket money of £80 to dollars. ....

(c) At the end of their holiday Mrs Campbell had 150 Canadian dollars left over.
Roughly how much is this in pounds? ....

(d) Mr Campbell bought a camera in Canada which cost him 225 Canadian dollars.
Approximately how much is this in pounds? ....

2  Use the graph to help you answer the questions below.

(a) A car's petrol tank holds 8 gallons. How many litres is this?

....

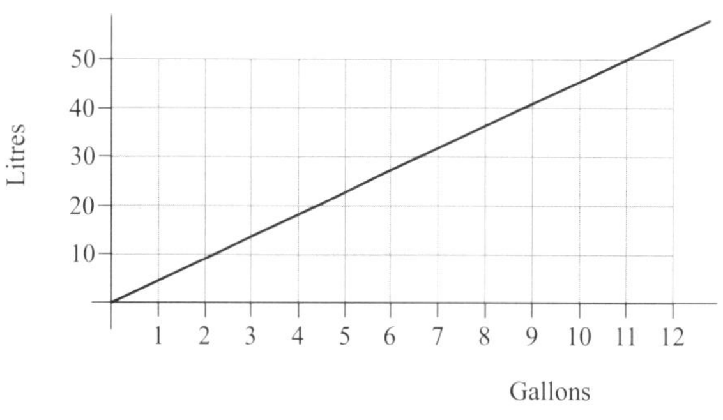

(b) Approximately how many litres of water would fit into a 3 gallon container?

....

(c) The Jensens' paddling pool holds 40 litres of water. What is this in gallons?

....

3  R.B.Wheeler hires out bicycles. He charges a one-off fee of £5, plus £2 per day.
Use the graph to answer the following questions.

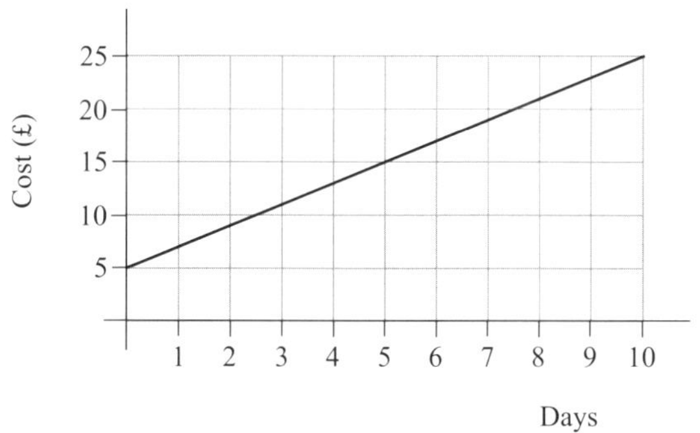

(a) You want to hire a bicycle for 8 days.
How much will you have to pay?

....

(b) Andy hired a bicycle on holiday.
He paid £15.
How long did he hire the bike for?

....

Conversion Factors

1 If £1 is equal to 1.4 euros, how much is:

(a) £25 in euros?

....

(b) 84 euros in pounds?

....

2 K2 is the second highest mountain in the world. It is 8610 metres high. What is this in kilometres?

....

3 A gorilla weighs 0.35 tonnes. How many kilograms is this?

....

4 Jay is 1.78 metres tall.

(a) How many centimetres is this?

....

His cat, Alfie, is 0.28 m high.

(b) How tall is Alfie in cm?

....

5 Alice's hamster is getting fat. At the moment it weighs 0.4 of a pound. How many ounces is this? (Hint: There are 16 ounces in a pound.)

....

Working with Fractions

1  Work out the following:

(a) $\frac{1}{2} \times \frac{1}{6}$ ....

(b) $\frac{1}{4} \times \frac{3}{4}$ ....

(c) $\frac{2}{5} \times \frac{3}{7}$ ....

(d) $\frac{2}{9} \times \frac{2}{1}$ ....

2 Work out the following. Cancel your answers so that they are in their simplest form.

(a) $\frac{1}{4} \times \frac{2}{3}$ ....

(b) $\frac{2}{3} \times \frac{3}{5}$ ....

(c) $\frac{2}{9} \times \frac{3}{4}$ ....

(d) $\frac{3}{10} \times \frac{5}{6}$ ....

3 These questions involve mixed fractions.

E.g. $\frac{1}{4} \times 2\frac{1}{2} = \frac{1}{4} \times \frac{5}{2} = \frac{5}{8}$

Give your answers in their simplest form.

(a) $\frac{1}{2} \times 1\frac{1}{4}$ ....

(b) $\frac{2}{5} \times 1\frac{1}{2}$ ....

(c) $\frac{3}{4} \times 2\frac{1}{5}$ ....

4 Work out the following:

(a) $\frac{1}{2} \div \frac{1}{6}$ ....

(b) $\frac{1}{4} \div \frac{3}{4}$ ....

(c) $\frac{2}{3} \div \frac{3}{5}$ ....

(d) $\frac{4}{9} \div 2$ ....

Working with Fractions

1  Work out the answers to the following:

(a) $\frac{2}{5} + \frac{1}{5}$ ....

(b) $\frac{2}{8} + \frac{3}{8}$ ....

(c) $\frac{4}{9} - \frac{2}{9}$ ....

(d) $\frac{3}{4} - \frac{1}{4}$ ....

2  Write down the number that could go in the box for each equation below.

(a) $\frac{1}{2} = \frac{\square}{20}$ ....

(b) $\frac{3}{5} = \frac{\square}{15}$ ....

(c) $\frac{1}{4} = \frac{\square}{8}$ ....

(d) $\frac{2}{3} = \frac{\square}{18}$ ....

(e) $\frac{3}{5} = \frac{\square}{20}$ ....

(f) $\frac{3}{4} = \frac{\square}{12}$ ....

3  This is a question about adding and subtracting fractions.

(a) Put each pair of fractions over a common denominator. The first one is already done.

(i) $\frac{2}{3}$ and $\frac{1}{2}$ $\frac{4}{6}$ and $\frac{3}{6}$

(ii) $\frac{1}{4}$ and $\frac{2}{5}$ ....

(iii) $\frac{4}{5}$ and $\frac{2}{3}$ ....

(iv) $\frac{3}{5}$ and $\frac{1}{2}$ ....

(v) $\frac{2}{7}$ and $\frac{3}{4}$ ....

(vi) $\frac{1}{6}$ and $\frac{2}{3}$ ....

(b) Now work out the answers to the following, using your answers to part (a):

(i) $\frac{2}{3} + \frac{1}{2}$ ....

(ii) $\frac{1}{4} + \frac{2}{5}$ ....

(iii) $\frac{4}{5} - \frac{2}{3}$ ....

(iv) $\frac{3}{5} - \frac{1}{2}$ ....

(v) $\frac{2}{7} + \frac{3}{4}$ ....

(vi) $\frac{1}{6} - \frac{2}{3}$ ....

4  Work out the following:

(a) $\frac{3}{7} + \frac{2}{5}$ ....

(b) $\frac{5}{6} + \frac{3}{4}$ ....

Working with Fractions

1 Find the answers to the following:

(a) $\frac{1}{4}$ of £36 ....

(b) $\frac{1}{5}$ of 20 kg ....

(c) $\frac{1}{6}$ of 24 cm ....

(d) $\frac{3}{4}$ of 36 m ....

(e) $\frac{2}{5}$ of 20 litres ....

(f) $\frac{5}{6}$ of 24 pupils ....

2 Aunt Ida gave the three Crossland children £150 to share between them.

(a) Michael, the eldest, was to have $\frac{1}{2}$. What was his share?

....

(b) How much did Jilly get if her share was $\frac{1}{3}$?

....

(c) What fraction of the money is left over for Priscilla? How much does Priscilla get?

....

3 The turnout at last Saturday's Norwich City game was 12 400.

(a) $\frac{1}{4}$ were boys. How many boys were there? ....

(b) $\frac{1}{5}$ of the spectators were female. How many females were there? ....

(c) Season ticket holders made up $\frac{3}{8}$ of the crowd.

How many season ticket holders were there? ....

4 Mr Hanratty owns a farm. It covers 36 acres. He uses $\frac{5}{12}$ of his land for wheat. $\frac{1}{3}$ of the land has cows grazing on it. $\frac{1}{6}$ of the land is used to house his pigs. The remaining $\frac{1}{12}$ of the land is taken up by the farmhouse.

Work out how many acres are taken up by:

wheat ....

cows ....

pigs ....

farmhouse ....

Fractions, Decimals and Percentages

1 Change the following decimals to fractions:

(a) 0.9 .... (b) 0.09 .... (c) 0.23 ....

(d) 0.6 .... (e) 0.06 .... (f) 0.15 ....

(g) 0.28 ....

2 Convert the following fractions to decimals:

(a) $\frac{1}{2}$ .... (b) $\frac{3}{4}$ .... (c) $\frac{2}{5}$ ....

(d) $\frac{5}{8}$ .... (e) $\frac{7}{10}$ .... (f) $\frac{7}{100}$ ....

(g) $\frac{55}{100}$ .... (h) $\frac{9}{20}$ .... (i) $\frac{1}{3}$ ....

(j) $\frac{2}{9}$ ....

3  Three friends scored the following marks in a test: Ria $\frac{15}{20}$, Annie $\frac{18}{20}$, Liz $\frac{12}{20}$
Convert each person's mark into a percentage.

Ria ....

Annie ....

Liz ....

4  Just before half-term Steve did three tests and got the following marks:

English $\frac{18}{30}$, French $\frac{27}{50}$, History $\frac{16}{20}$.

Turn each of his scores into a percentage.

English: .... French: .... History: ....

5  Fill in the missing values in the table:

	Fraction	Decimal	Percentage
(a)	$\frac{3}{10}$		
(b)		0.625	
(c)			80%
(d)	$\frac{7}{20}$		

Percentages

1 A family bought a suitcase for their holidays.
The price ticket on the suitcase was £18, but there was a discount of 10% off this price.
What did they pay for the case?

....

....

....

2 Paul hires a car for his holiday. The cost is £150 + VAT, where VAT is charged at 17.5%.
Find the total amount paid for the car.

....

....

3 A student has borrowed £500 from a bank. The bank charges 6% interest per year. How much interest does the student owe the bank at the end of one year?
(Assume he pays no money back in the first year.)

Student Bank Loans:
Interest rate —
Only 6% per annum

....

....

4 Charley bought a car last year. Since then its value has decreased by 12%.
The car cost £4500. What is the value of the car now?

....

....

5 A packet of biscuits usually contains 500 g. A special offer packet contains an extra 20% free.
How much does the special offer packet contain?

....

....

Percentages

1 A supermarket buys crisps for 16p per packet and sells them for 20p per packet.
What is the profit as a percentage?

....

....

2 A student earns £125 a week. She spends £30 a week on food.
What percentage of her wage does she spend on food?

....

....

3 In a 40 g serving of cereal there is 6 g of sugar. What percentage of the cereal is sugar?

....

....

4 The table below shows the results of a survey among some Year 3 children.

Favourite colour	White	Red	Blue	Green	Yellow	Other
Boys	4	9	2	3	0	2
Girls	3	5	7	2	5	3

(a) What percentage of the boys chose red as their favourite colour?

....

(b) What percentage of the children chose blue as their favourite colour?

....

5 A box of chocolates contains milk, plain and white chocolates.
There are 14 milk chocolates, 18 plain chocolates and 8 white chocolates.

What percentage of the chocolates are milk chocolates?

....

More Numbers Mini-Exam (1)

1 The tallest boy in a school is 1.95 m tall.

(a) What is his height in centimetres?

....

(b) Approximately how tall is he in feet and inches?

....

....

2  (a) There were 48 459 people at a football match. Give this figure to 2 significant figures.

....

(b) The diameter of the football used in the match was 22.7 cm. What is this to the nearest cm?

....

3  Estimate the value of $\frac{37 \times 296}{58}$.

....

....

4 This is a graph to convert between pounds (£) and euros (€).

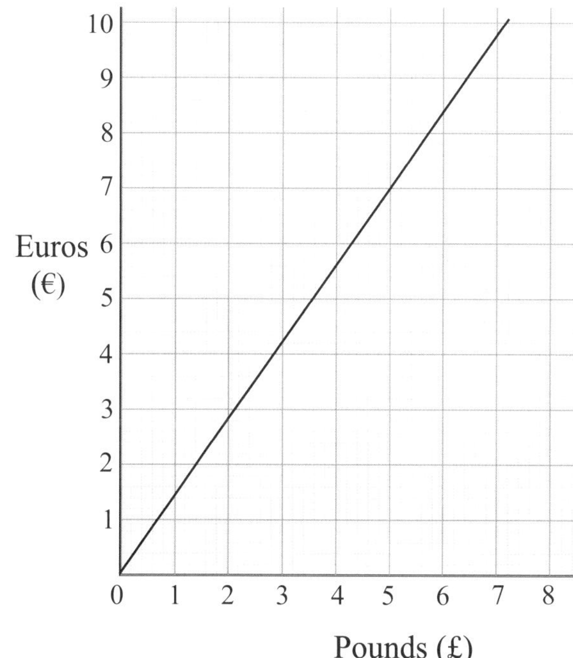

(a) Use the graph to estimate:

(i) how much €8 is worth in pounds.

....

(ii) how much £3.30 is worth in euros.

....

(b) A train ticket costs £70.
How much is this in euros?

....

....

....

More Numbers Mini-Exam (1)

5  Calculate:

(a) $\frac{3}{4} \times \frac{2}{5}$ ....

(b) $\frac{3}{4} - \frac{2}{5}$ ....

(c) $\frac{3}{4} \div \frac{2}{5}$ ....

6  Complete the table below:

Fraction	Decimal	Percentage
$^{9}/_{10}$		
	0.19	
		25%

Put the values 9/10, 0·19 and 25% in order, starting with the smallest.

....

7  This is a question about fractions.

(a) Find $\frac{3}{4}$ of 28 m.

....

(b) A school library has £60 to spend on books. They must spend $\frac{4}{5}$ of the money on non-fiction books. How much must they spend on non-fiction books?

....

8 A computer normally costs £850, but there is a discount of 10% in a sale.

(a) What is the sale price of the computer?

....

A printer for the computer costs £120, but this has a discount of 15% in the sale.

(b) What is the sale price of the printer?

....

More Numbers Mini-Exam (2)

1 A suitcase weighs 9.5 kg. How heavy is the suitcase in lbs?
Give your answer to the nearest lb. Use the conversion factor 1 kg = 2.2 lbs.

....

2 A snake measures 72 cm. How long is the snake in inches?
Give your answer to the nearest inch. Use the conversion factor 1 inch = 2·5 cm.

....

3 The exchange rate for converting between US dollars and UK pounds is £1 = US $1.6.

(a) James wants to change £150 into dollars for his holiday. How many dollars will he get?

....

(b) The charge for entry into a theme park is $20. How much is this in pounds and pence?

....

4 The distance from London to Glasgow is 412 miles. How far is this in kilometres?
Give your answer to the nearest kilometre. Use the conversion factor 1 mile = 1.6 km.

....

5 Drink containers come in many shapes and sizes.

(a) Cartons of cola come in packs of 6, giving a total of 1980 ml.
How many litres is this?

....

(b) Roughly how many pints are there in a 1 litre carton of milk?

....

(c) Wine bottles usually contain 75 cl of wine. This is equivalent to 0.75 litres.
How much is this in gallons? (Give your answer to 2 decimal places.)

....

More Numbers Mini-Exam (2)

6 This question is about fractions, decimals and percentages.

(a) Write these fractions as decimals:

(i) $\frac{9}{20}$ ....

(ii) $\frac{3}{8}$ ....

(b) Put these values in order starting with the smallest:

$\mathbf{\frac{3}{8}}$ **0.29** $\mathbf{\frac{9}{20}}$ **40%**

....

7 Calculate $\frac{3}{7}$ of 1750 m. Give your answer in kilometres.

....

8 A jug contains 3 litres of a mixture of lemon and lime squash.

Calculate the amount of lemon squash in the jug if 55% of the jug's contents is lime squash. Give your answer in millilitres.

....

....

9 The cost of a garden shed is £110 + VAT, where VAT is charged at 17.5%.

What is the total cost of the shed?

....

....

10 In a box of 350 apples, 14 are found to be rotten.

What percentage of the apples are rotten?

....

....

Mean, Median, Mode and Range

1 Charlotte asked 11 of her friends how many television sets they had in their house.
Her results were:

4 2 3 3 1 4 3 3 2 6 2

(a) Write down the mode.

....

(b) What is the median number of television sets?

....

....

(c) Work out the mean number of television sets.

....

....

2 The list below shows how many bottles a family recycled each week over a period of 8 weeks:

10 12 3 7 4 6 7 11

(a) Work out the range of the number of bottles.

....

....

(b) Calculate the mean number of recycled bottles.

....

....

3 Ben counted cars for his geography coursework. He stood at the roadside for an hour and made a note of how many cars passed him every 10 minutes. His results were:

24 26 30 27 35 29

(a) What is the median number of cars that passed Ben in 10 minutes?

....

....

(b) Work out the mean number of cars per 10 minutes.

....

....

Mean, Median, Mode and Range

1 A small company employs 5 people.
Their annual salaries are listed below:

£18 000 £38 500 £18 000 £25 200 £18 000

(a) Write down the mode.

....

(b) What is the median annual salary?

....

(c) Calculate the mean annual salary.

....

2 A group of 8 friends enjoy skating, but they often break their skateboards.
Each friend says how many skateboards he or she has broken this year.
The results are given below:

6 4 5 8 8 3 8 4

(a) Work out the range.

....

(b) What is the mode?

....

(c) What is the median number of broken skateboards?

....

3 One evening Preya makes 10 phone calls. When the bill comes it shows how long each call was, in minutes. The call lengths are listed below:

10 12 25 3 37 13 12 18 41 33

(a) Work out the median length of Preya's calls.

....

(b) Calculate the mean phone call length.

....

....

(c) What is the range?

....

Frequency Tables

1 

Tom thinks that most people's favourite colours are red, blue or yellow. He conducts a small survey to see if he is right. He asks the question, "Which is your favourite colour — red, blue, yellow or a different colour?" The replies are:

Blue **Red** **Other** **Red** **Red**
Yellow **Red** **Blue** **Blue** **Other**
Blue **Red** **Yellow** **Other** **Red**
Other **Red** **Other** **Yellow** **Blue**

(a) Use tallies to complete the table:

Colour	Tally	Frequency
Red		
Blue		
Yellow		
Other		

(b) Which colour is the mode?

....

2 Gemma asks 10 of her friends how many CDs they own. The results are shown in the table:

Number of CDs	Tally	Frequency
0-19	II	
20-39	IIII	
40 and over	IIII	

Later she asks 10 more friends. Their replies were:

17 33 51 27 42 12 37 46 22 29

Add the results from the additional 10 friends to the tally sheet and complete the frequency column.

Bar Charts

1  The number of pairs of trainers owned by players in a school football squad are shown in the bar chart below:

(a) What is the modal number of pairs of trainers?

....

(b) Work out the range.

....

(c) How many players were in the football squad?

....

2 The frequency table shows how much pocket money each pupil in a class of 10-year-olds received each week:

Amount of Pocket Money (x)	Number of Pupils
£0 ≤ x < £1	5
£1 ≤ x < £2	13
£2 ≤ x < £3	8
£3 ≤ x < £4	3
£4 ≤ x < £5	1

(a) Draw a bar chart to show the amount of pocket money received.

Number of Pupils: 0, 5, 10, 15

Amount of pocket money (£): 0, 1, 2, 3, 4, 5

(b) What is the mode?

....

Line Graphs and Two-way Tables

1  The grouped frequency table below shows the number of hours of homework 30 students did in one week.

Hours of Homework	0 to 2	2 to 4	4 to 6	6 to 8
Frequency	15	7	5	3

Draw a frequency polygon for the data.

2 This two-way table shows the number of adults and the number of children living in houses on Avenue Road:

		Number of Adults				
		1	**2**	**3**	**4**	**Total**
Number of Children	**0**	1	1	1	1	
	1	2	2	1	0	
	2	2	5	0	0	
	3	0	2	0	0	
	4	0	1	0	0	
	Total					

(a) Complete the table to show the totals for each of the rows and columns.

(b) How many houses had 2 adults and 3 children living in them? ....

(c) How many houses had 2 children living in them? ....

(d) How many houses were there on Avenue Road? ....

Pictograms and Stem & Leaf Diagrams

1 This pictogram shows the number of jars of jam sold in a campsite shop.

Strawberry Jam	
Blackberry Jam	
Raspberry jam	
	Represents 10 jars

(a) How many jars of strawberry jam were sold?

....

(b) The shop sold 35 jars of raspberry jam. Complete the pictogram.

(c) How many jars of jam were sold altogether by the shop?

....

2  The heights of 20 students in a class were measured to the nearest cm. The results are below:

165	163	159	171	162	167	155	158	173	169
169	159	172	175	171	169	163	160	164	170

(a) Draw a stem and leaf diagram to illustrate the data.

(b) How tall is the tallest person in the class?

....

(c) What is the range of the heights?

....

(d) What is the mode?

....

3  Joe asked his friends how many computer games they had. Their replies are shown below:

20 53 23 88 76 32 37 19 26 39 52 61 55 81 29

(a) Draw a stem and leaf diagram to illustrate the data.

(b) What is the median number of computer games?

....

Scatter Graphs and Correlation

1  A survey of 10 people was carried out. They were asked how many hours they watched TV and how many hours they listened to the radio each week. This scatter graph shows the results.

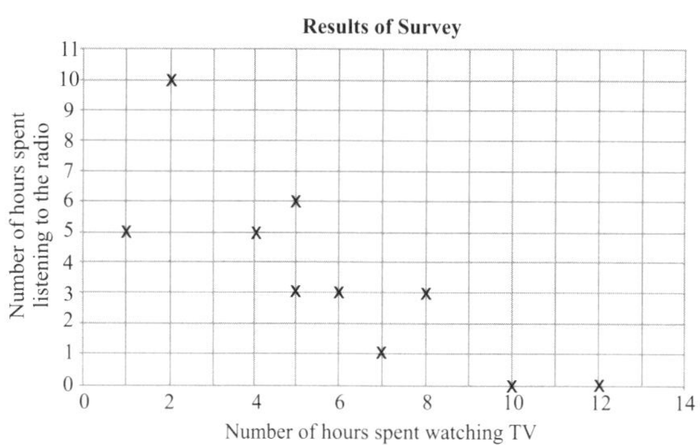

(a) Draw a line of best fit on the scatter graph.

(b) Describe the relationship between the number of hours spent watching TV and the number of hours spent listening to the radio.

....

(c) Hilton listened to the radio for 5½ hours in the same week. Use your graph to estimate how much TV he watched.

....

2  The heights and weights of boys playing in a rugby team are shown in the table below.

Player	Height (cm)	Weight (kg)
1	170	71
2	168	69
3	179	75
4	165	66
5	161	60
6	172	71
7	180	77
8	177	72
9	173	70
10	176	75
11	173	68
12	168	67
13	169	70
14	183	76
15	176	Not known

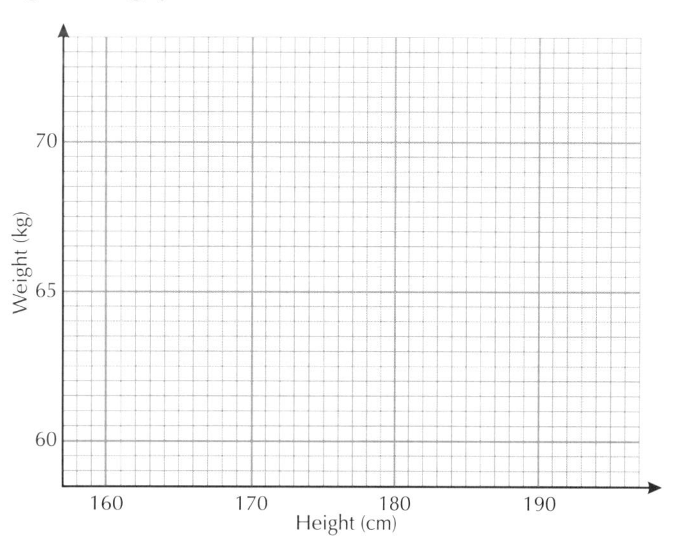

(a) Draw a scatter graph of the data for players 1 to 14.

(b) Draw a line of best fit on your graph.

(c) What can you say about the heights and weights?

....

(d) Use your graph to estimate the weight of player 15.

....

Pie Charts

1  120 people were interviewed outside a leisure centre. They were asked which sport they preferred to do in their leisure time.
The results are shown in the pie chart.

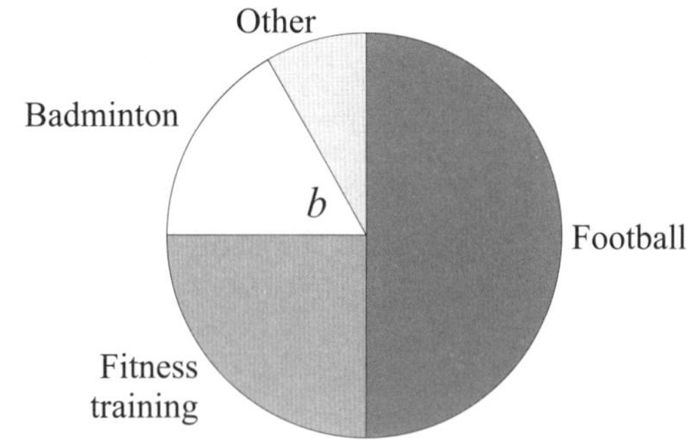

(a) What fraction of the people who were interviewed preferred to do fitness training?

....

(b) (i) Measure the angle marked b.

....

(ii) Use your answer to calculate how many people preferred to play badminton.

....

2 The sales of various drinks in a café were recorded for two different days.
The results are shown in the pie charts below.

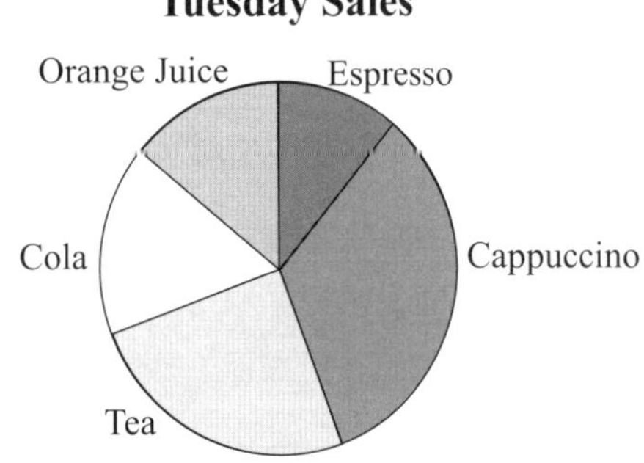

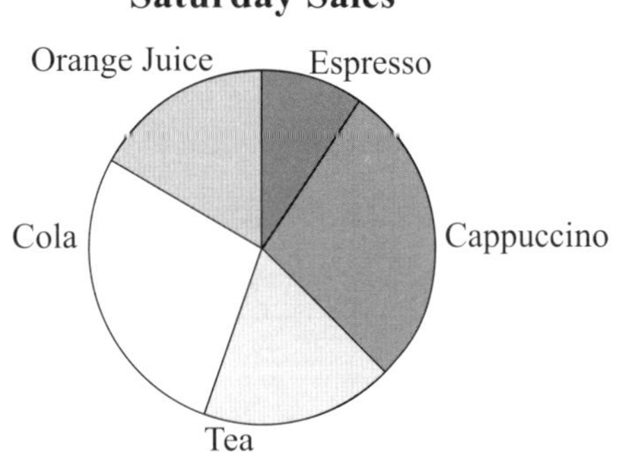

(a) What is the angle of the sector representing Tuesday's tea sales? ....

(b) What fraction of the drinks sold on Tuesday was tea? ....

(c) On which day was the greater proportion of tea sold? ....

On Tuesday the café sold 100 cappuccinos.

(d) How many drinks of cola were sold? ....

(e) The total number of drinks sold on Saturday was 600. How many of these were orange juice?

....

Probability

1 Add labels A, B, C and D to the arrows on the scale below to show the probabilities of the following events:

A a coin will land on its rim when tossed

B the next person to be born in the USA will be male

C you will watch television at least once this winter

D next time you throw a dice you get a six

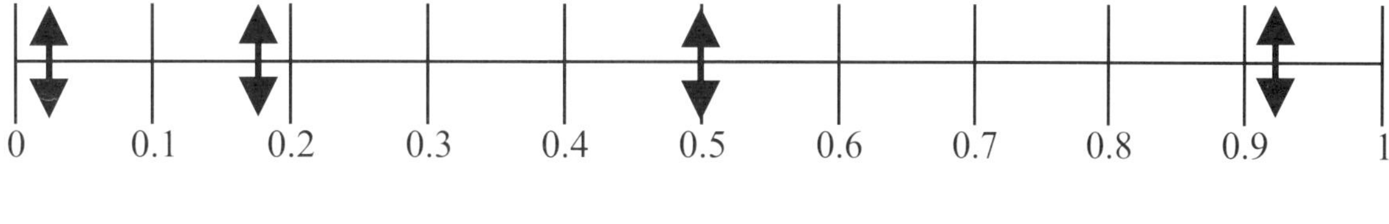

....

2 The 5-sided spinner shown is labelled with the numbers 1-5. It has an equal probability of landing on any of the numbers.

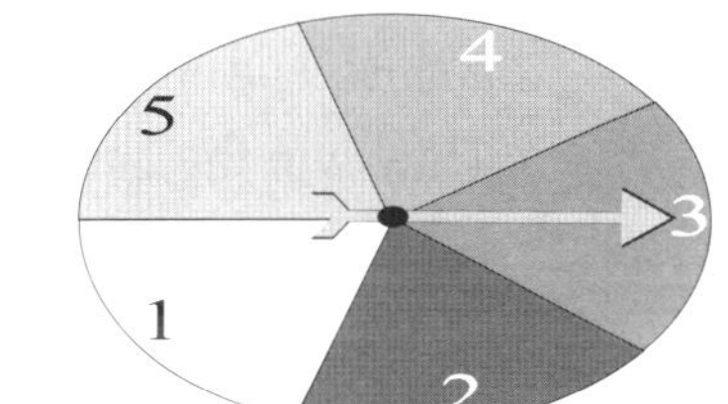

(a) What is the probability of the spinner landing on 1?

....

(b) What is the probability of the spinner landing on an even number?

....

3 A fair dice labelled 1-6 is thrown once.

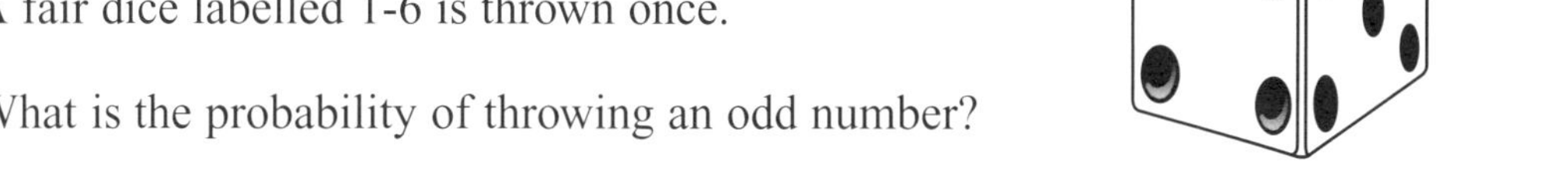

(a) What is the probability of throwing an odd number?

....

(b) What is the probability of throwing a 3?

....

(c) What is the probability of throwing a number bigger than 4?

....

Probability

1  This bar chart shows the numbers of different coloured counters in a bag.

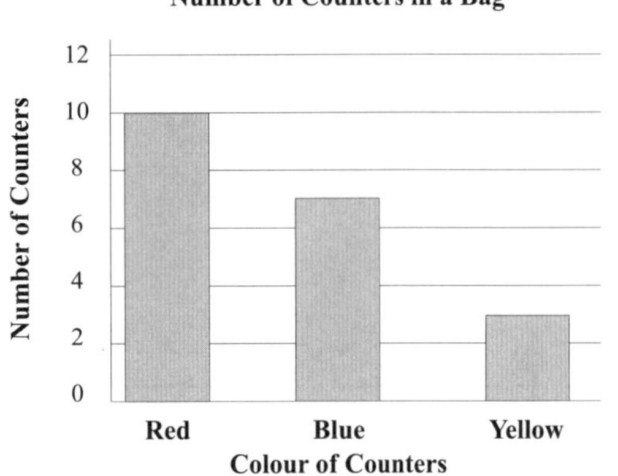

(a) How many counters are in the bag?

....

Anne takes one counter out of the bag at random and then puts it back.

(b) What is the probability that Anne chose a blue counter?

....

All the red counters are removed, and then Dave takes out a counter.

(c) What is the probability that the counter Dave takes out is yellow?

....

2 Ashish and Sue are playing a game where they have to spin the spinner in the picture. They win the amount the arrow points to.

(a) What is the probability that Ashish wins £2?

....

(b) What is the probability that Sue wins £2 or more?

....

3 The probabilities of Ashby Rovers football team winning, drawing or losing a match **at home** are given in the following table:

Winning	Drawing	Losing
$\frac{2}{8}$	$\frac{3}{8}$	$\frac{3}{8}$

(a) What is the probability of Ashby Rovers winning a home match? Give your answer in its simplest form.

....

(b) What is the probability that they **either** win **or** draw a home match?

....

If they play a match away from home, the probability that they will win is halved.

(c) What is the probability of them winning an **away** match?

....

Probability

1  There are blue, red and green toy bricks in a bag. When a brick is picked out at random, the probability of it being blue is 0.3 and the probability of it being green is 0.2.

(a) What is the probability of picking out a red brick?

....

There are 40 bricks in the bag.

(b) How many of the bricks are green?

....

2  John has a fair coin. He also has a fair spinner, which is equally likely to show 1, 2 or 3. He spins the spinner and tosses the coin.

(a) Complete the table to show all the possible outcomes.

Coin	Spinner
Head	2

(b) Write down the probability that John gets a 3 and a tail.

....

3  What is the probability of not getting a 5 or a 6 on a roll of a fair dice?

....

Graphs

1  Use the grid to answer the questions that follow.

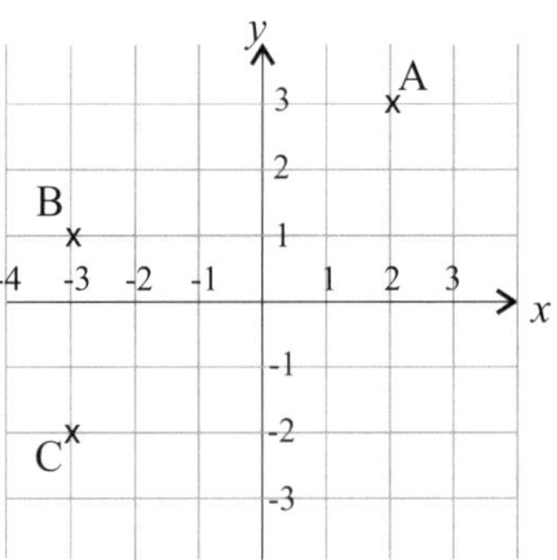

Write down the coordinates of:

(a) Point A

....

(b) Point B

....

(c) Point C

....

The point D could also be plotted on the above diagram, so that the shape ABCD forms a parallelogram.

(d) Write down the coordinates of point D.

....

2 You need to use the grid below for this question.

(a) Plot the following points: **A** (0, 1) **B** (2, 1) **C** (3, –2) **D** (0, –1) and join them to form a quadrilateral.

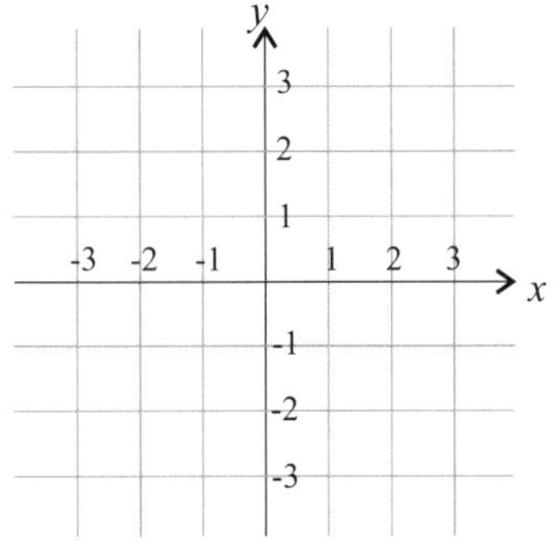

(b) What is the name of the shape you have drawn?

....

Drawing Graphs from Equations

1  Draw the following lines on the axes on the right:

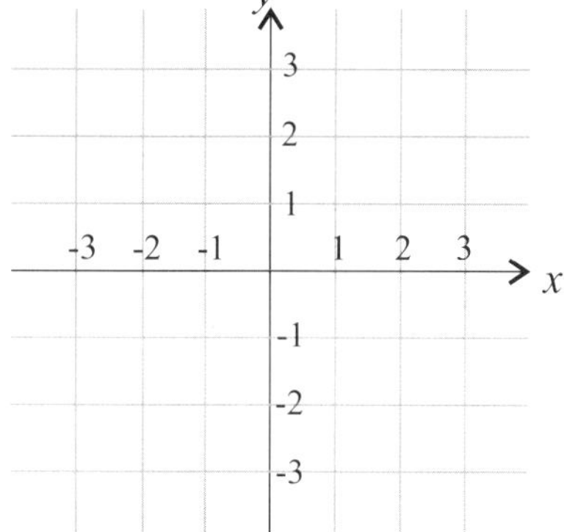

(a) $y = 3$

(b) $x = -2$

(c) $y = x$

(d) What are the coordinates of the point where the lines $y = 3$ and $y = x$ meet?

....

2  Use this grid to answer the questions that follow:

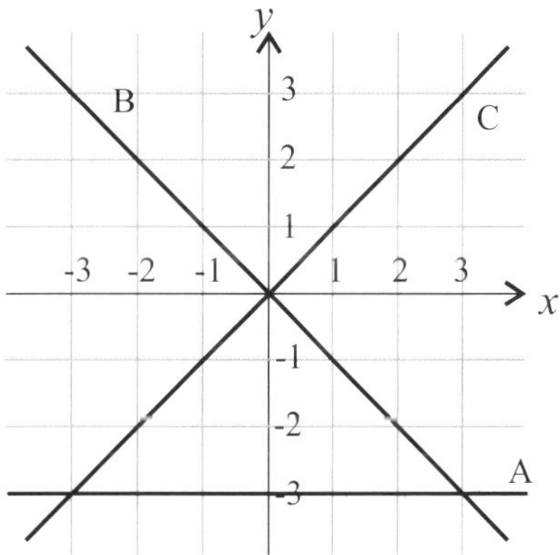

(a) Give the equation of line A on the diagram above.

....

(b) Give the equation of line B on the diagram above.

....

(c) What is the area of the triangle formed by lines A, B and C?

....

Drawing Graphs from Equations

1  This question is all about plotting a graph.

(a) Complete this table of values using the equation $y = 3x - 2$

x	-2	-1	0	1	2
y					

(b) Use your table of values to plot the graph of $y = 3x - 2$ on the grid below.

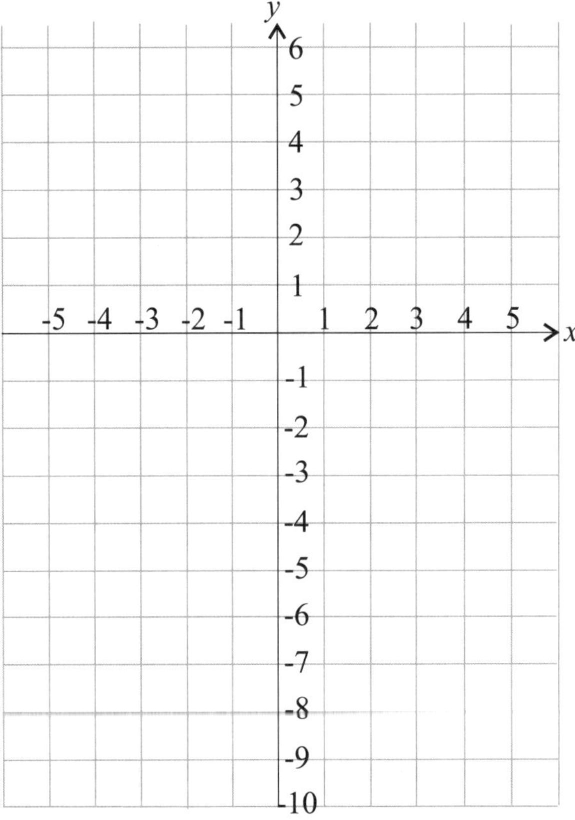

(c) On the same grid, plot the graph of $y = -2x + 2$.
Use the space below for your working.

Finding the Midpoint of a Line

1  On the grid below plot the points **A** (2, 1), **B** (4, 3) and **C** (6, –3).

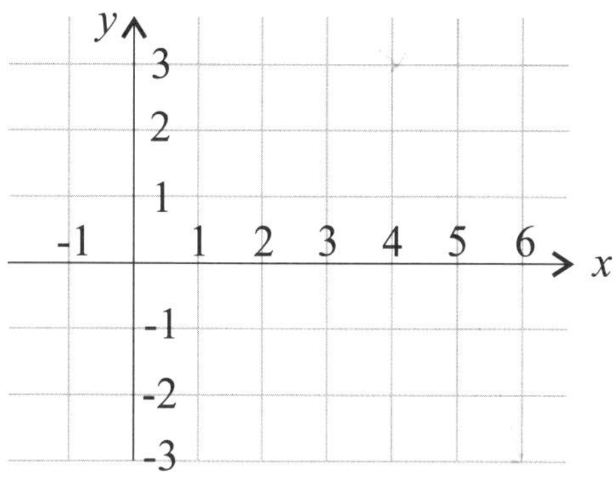

(a) Find the midpoint of the line **AB**.

....

(b) Find the midpoint of the line **AC**.

....

2  Points A and B have been plotted on the grid below:

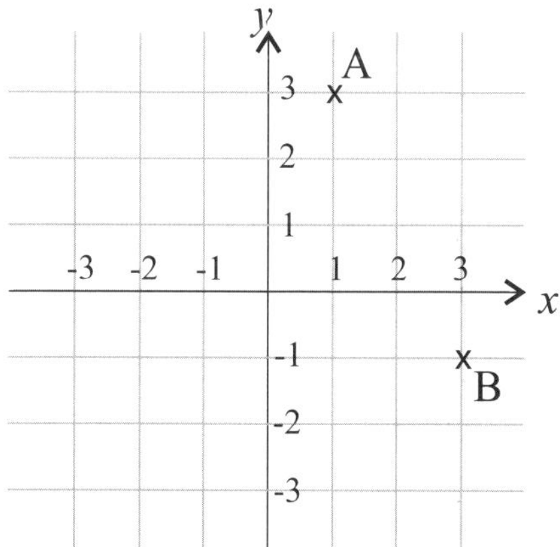

(a) Find the midpoint of the line AB.

....

(b) Add the line $y = x$ to the diagram.

(c) Give the equation of a vertical line through B.

....

....

Statistics and Graphs Mini-Exam (1)

1  Some children played a game using a fair spinner like the one shown below.
Mark with an X the probability of obtaining each colour when the spinner is spun once.
Use the probability lines below.

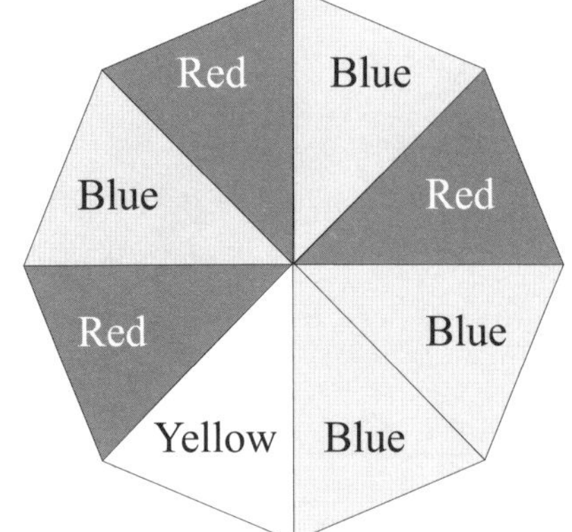

(a) Blue: 0 ——————— 1

(b) Yellow: 0 ——————— 1

(c) White: 0 ——————— 1

2  Look at this chart showing the amount of litter dropped in Newtown-under-the-Willows.
A local councillor claims that the litter problem in the town is getting dramatically worse.
Give TWO reasons why this diagram might be misleading.

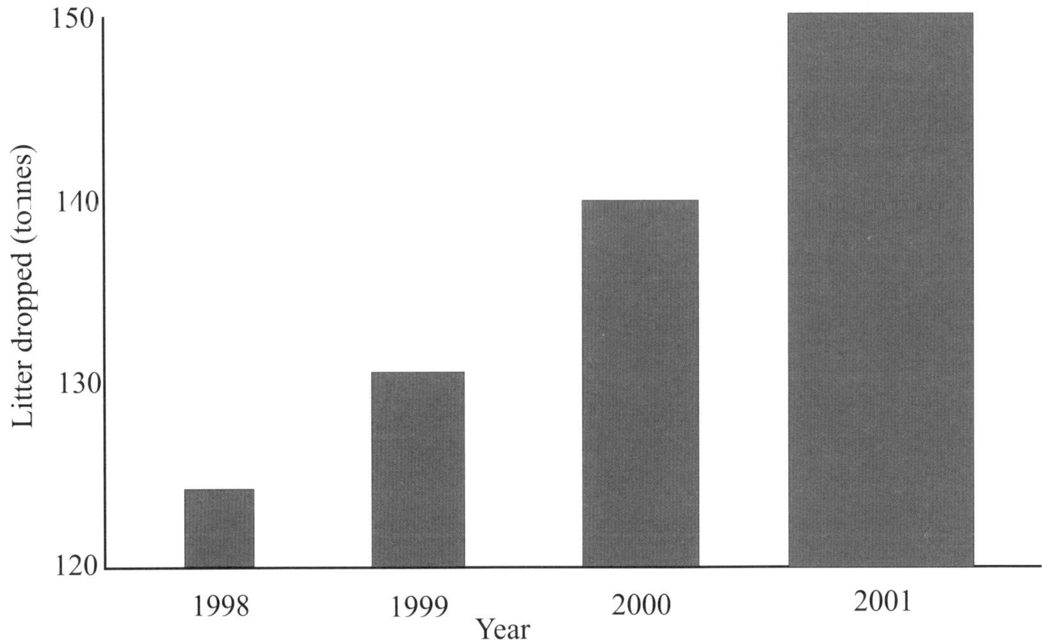

Reason 1:

....

Reason 2:

....

Statistics and Graphs Mini-Exam (1)

3  P, Q and R are 3 points on a 1 cm grid.

(a) Write down the coordinates of the point Q.

....

(b) Given that PQRS is a parallelogram, mark and label the point S.

(c) Draw a line through R parallel to the x-axis. Give the equation of the line you have drawn.

....

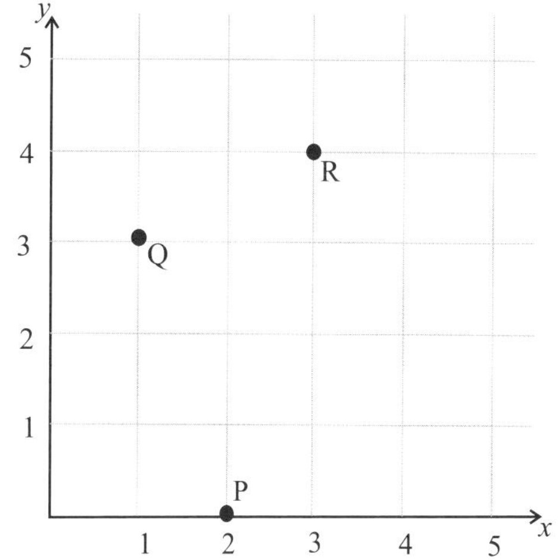

4  Julie recorded the height and arm length (in cm) of 10 girls in her form.

Height	170	180	167	152	163	172	165	174	185	192
Arm Length	90	95	89	84	85	90	95	90	92	94

(a) Complete this scatter diagram to show the results. The first 3 points are already plotted.

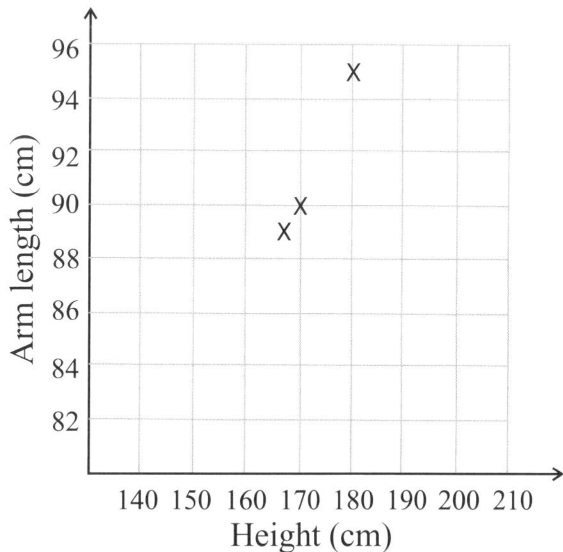

(b) Comment on the relationship between height and arm length for these girls.

....

Statistics and Graphs Mini-Exam (2)

1  A student scored the following marks in his spelling tests:

8, 5, 4, 7, 3, 9, 4, 7, 6, 7

(a) Write down the mode of his marks.

....

(b) Find the median of his marks.

....

(c) Work out his mean mark.

....

2  Paula asked 180 girls what their favourite sport was. Here are her results:

Favourite Sport	**Number**
Football	37
Basketball	18
Tennis	25
Softball	74
Other	26

(a) Draw a pie chart to illustrate these results.

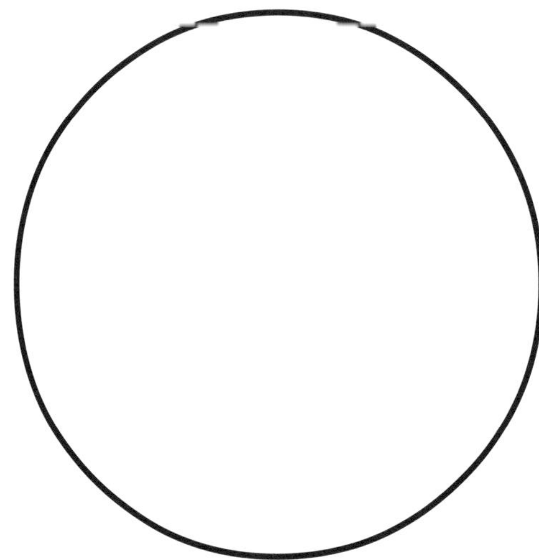

(b) Paula also asked 90 boys about their favourite sport and drew a pie chart to show her results. In this pie chart the angle for basketball was 64°. How many of the boys said that basketball was their favourite sport?

....

Statistics and Graphs Mini-Exam (2)

3  200 people were asked if they were right-handed or left-handed. The results are shown in the table, together with details about whether the people were male or female. Unfortunately some of the figures are missing.

	Left-Handed	Right-Handed	Total
Male	38		
Female		82	140
Total	96		200

(a) How many males took part in the survey?

....

(b) How many left-handed females took part in the survey?

....

(c) One of the 200 people is selected at random. What is the probability that:

(i) it will be a right-handed male?

....

(ii) it will not be a left-handed female?

....

4  The heights of twenty Year 9 students were measured in metres.
The measurements, to the nearest 0.01 m, are given below.

1.56 1.54 1.82 1.61 1.73 1.54 1.62 1.90 1.74 1.63
1.92 1.75 1.55 1.64 1.65 1.76 1.56 1.77 1.66 1.93

(a) Complete the frequency table below:

Height, h	Tally	Frequency
$1.50 < h \le 1.60$		
$1.60 < h \le 1.70$		
$1.70 < h \le 1.80$		
$1.80 < h \le 1.90$		
$1.90 < h \le 2.00$		

(b) Use the grid to draw a bar chart representing the information in the frequency table. Label your diagram clearly.

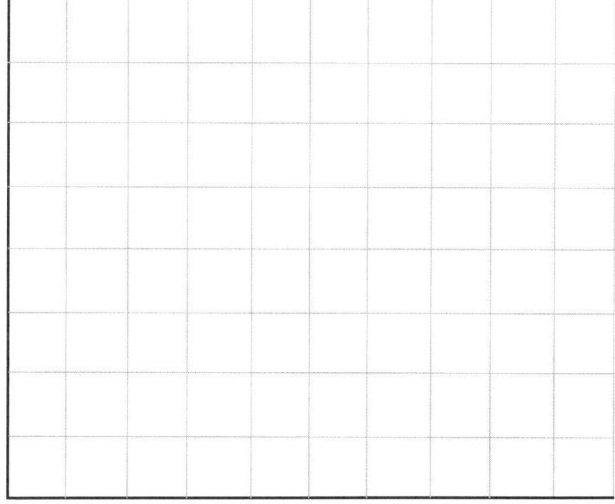

(c) One of these students is chosen at random. What is the probability that this student is taller than 1.80 m?

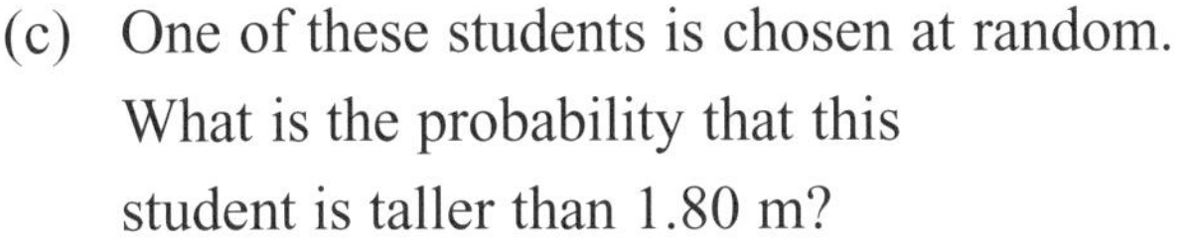

....

Time

1 A cake has to be baked for 2¼ hours. Pat puts the cake in the oven at 9.55 am.

What time should Pat take the cake out of the oven?

....

2 Priya is planning a train journey.

(a) It will take 25 minutes to get to the station and she wants to be there at 11:15.
By what time should she leave home?

....

(b) The train leaves at 11:35 and arrives at 13:22.
How long is the journey?

....

(c) Write 13:22 using the 12-hour clock.

....

3 A long-lasting lightbulb lasts 3000 hours.

If the light is left on all the time, how many days would this be?

....

....

4 A penguin once stayed underwater for 12 minutes and 28 seconds.
How many seconds is this?

....

Directions and Bearings

1 This is a plan of an adventure park.

N
Loop the Loop
Devil's Cauldron
Dragon Train
Space Trip
Thunder Ride
Water Splash

(a) Which ride is north-east of Space Trip?

....

(b) Which ride is west of Space Trip?

....

(c) If you stand at Devil's Cauldron and look towards Dragon Train, which direction are you looking in?

....

2 The diagram shows the positions of two telephone masts, X and Y.

(a) Measure and write down the bearing of Y from X.

....

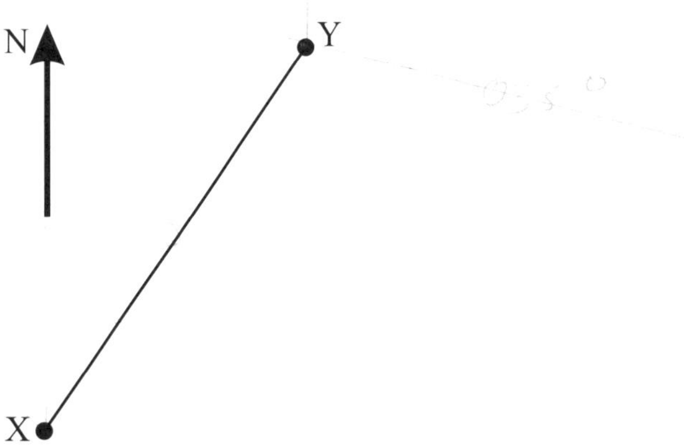

(b) Draw a line on the diagram pointing north-west from X.

(c) Draw a line on the diagram at a bearing of 100° from Y.

Maps and Map Scales

1  This map is drawn to a scale of 1 cm to 2 km.

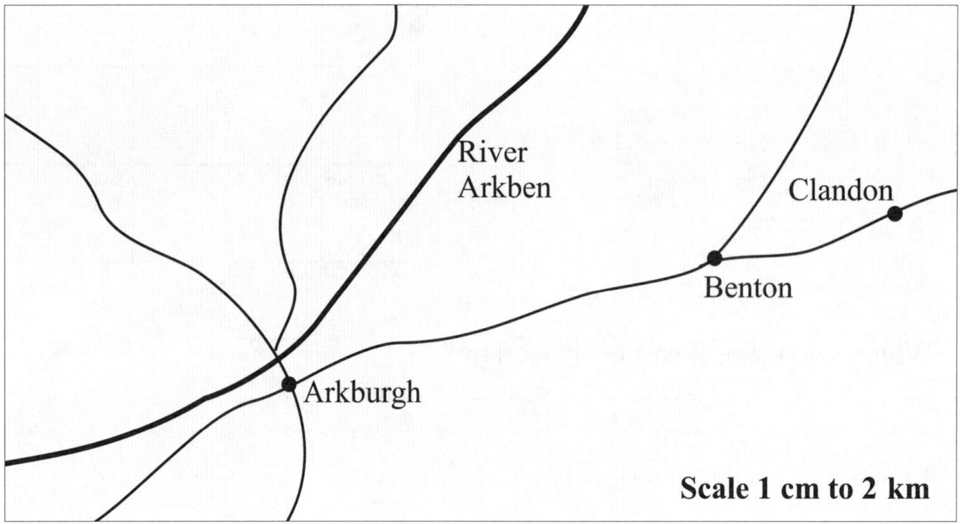

(a) Work out the actual distance between Arkburgh and Benton.

....

(b) What is the actual distance between Benton and Clandon?

....

(c) Joanna cycles 7 km to school. How far would this be on the map?

....

2 A plan of a park is drawn to a scale of 1 cm to 50 m.

(a) A path in the park is 450 m long. How long would the path be on the plan?

....

(b) A lake is 6 cm long on the plan. How long is the actual lake?

....

3 Below is a section of a map showing a railway line.

How far is Rinton from Hending?

....

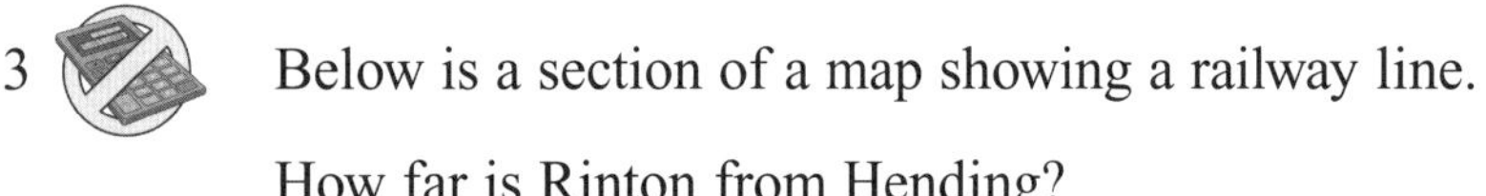

Travel Graphs and Speed

1 A man cycles at an average speed of 16 km/h for 2½ hours.
How far will he have travelled?

....

....

2 Calton and Didsburgh are towns 90 miles apart. At 12 o'clock midday Josh leaves Calton to travel to Didsburgh. This is a graph showing his journey to Didsburgh:

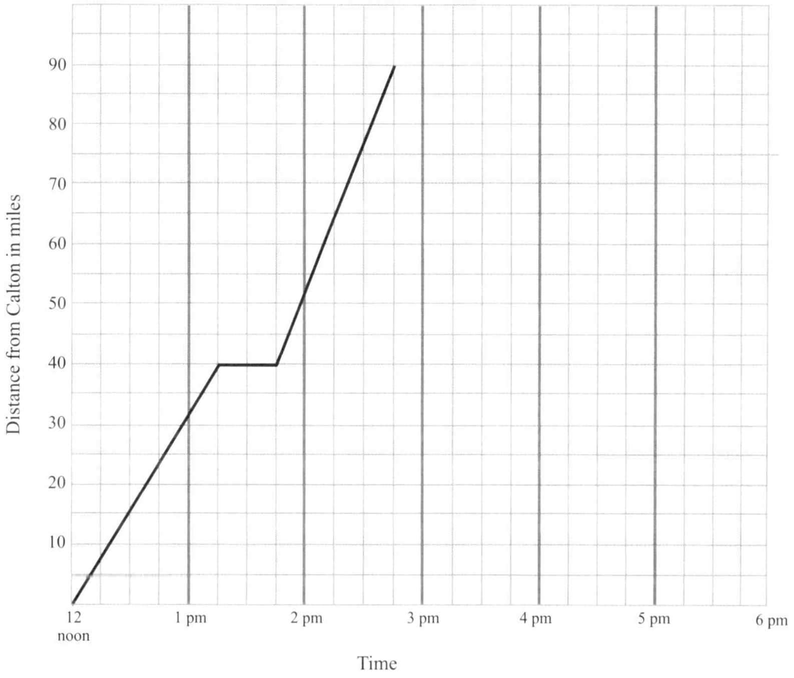

(a) How long did he take to complete the first 40 miles?

....

(b) What is happening at 1.30 pm?

....

(c) Between which times is he travelling fastest?

....

(d) Josh stays in Didsburgh for 1¼ hours, then travels straight back to Calton, arriving back at 6 pm. Complete the travel graph to show his stay in Didsburgh and his return journey.

....

(e) Josh takes 2 hours to travel 90 miles on his return journey.
What was his average speed for the return journey?

....

Lines and Angles

1  Look at the shape below.

(a) Put a cross on an obtuse angle in this diagram.

(b) Mark a reflex angle on the diagram.

2  A and B are two of the vertices of a triangle.

(a) Measure the angle at A.

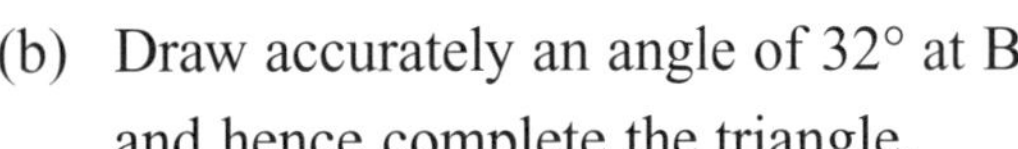

(b) Draw accurately an angle of 32° at B and hence complete the triangle.

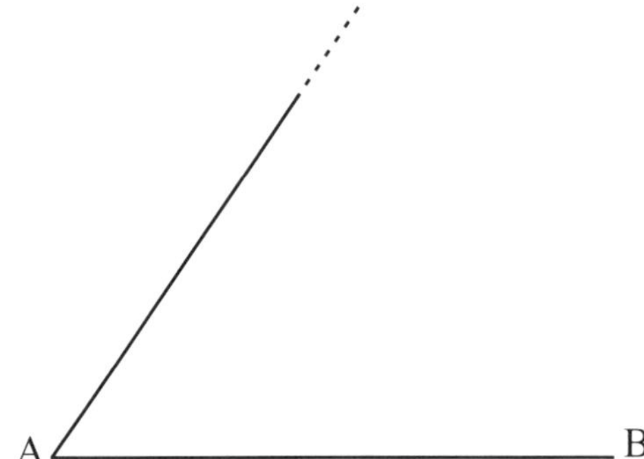

3 Measure all the internal angles of this quadrilateral.

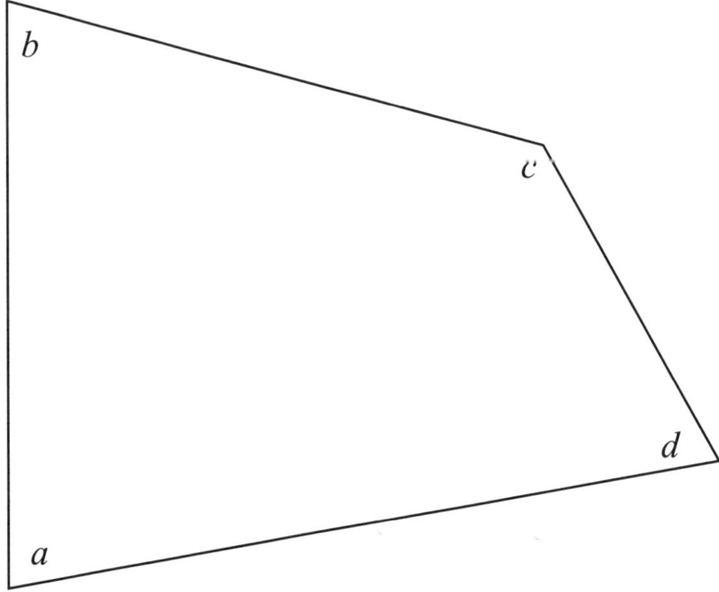

$a =$ .... $b =$ ....

$c =$ .... $d =$ ....

Five Angle Rules

1  Look at the shape below.

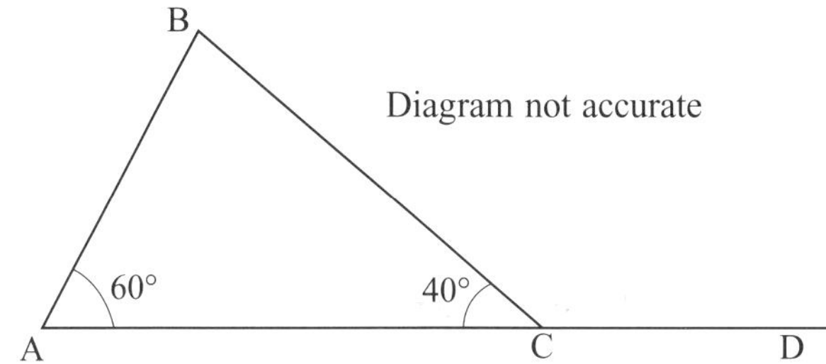

(a) Work out the size of angle ABC.

....

(b) Work out the size of angle BCD.

....

2  Look at the kite shape on the right.

(a) Calculate angle PSR.

....

(b) Calculate angle PQR.

....

Q
P 115° 115° R
S
110° 200°
T
Diagram not accurate

3  Look the the triangle drawn below.

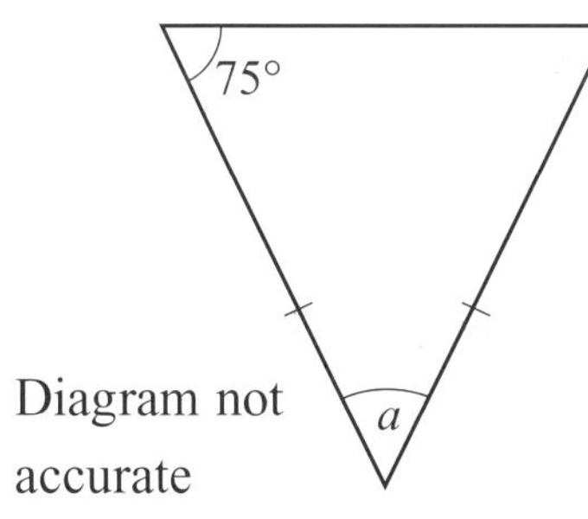

(a) What name is given to this type of triangle?

....

(b) Work out the size of angle a.

....

4  The quadrilateral UVXY is made up of two triangles.

(a) Find angle XVY.

....

(b) Find angle XYU.

....

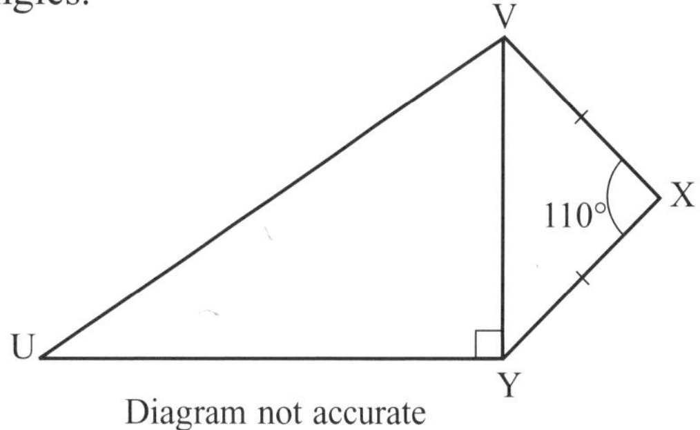

Parallel Lines

1  Look at the diagram on the right.

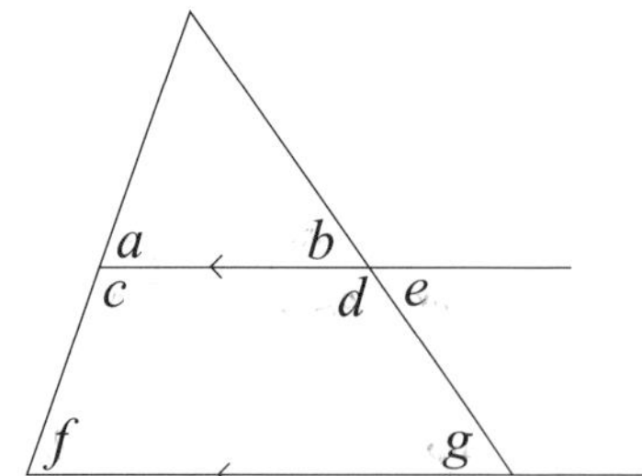

(a) Write down an angle equal to b.

....

(b) Write down a pair of angles that add to 180°.

....

2  The diagram below shows two parallel lines and a line that crosses them both.

75°
r
s

Diagram not accurate

(a) Write down the size of angle r.

....

(b) Circle the word below that describes the pair of angles marked r and 75°.

Alternate **Supplementary** **Corresponding**

(c) Write down the size of angle s.

....

3 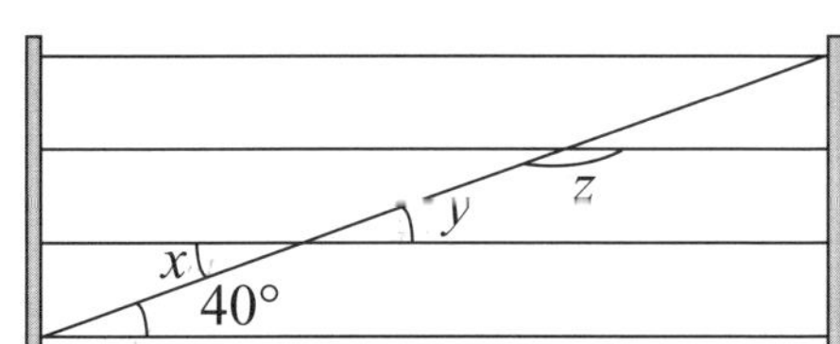

Diagram not accurate

The gate on the right has four parallel bars.
Write down the size of:

(a) angle x

....

(b) angle y

....

(c) angle z

....

4  ABCD is a quadrilateral.

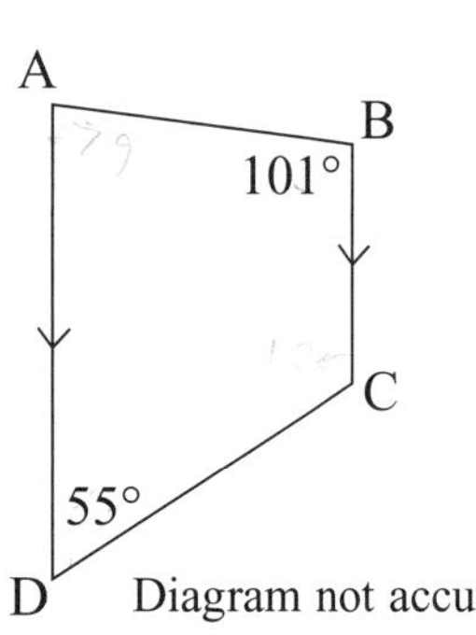

Diagram not accurate

(a) Work out angle BAD.

....

(b) Work out angle BCD.

....

....

Congruence and Similarity

1  Look at the shapes below.

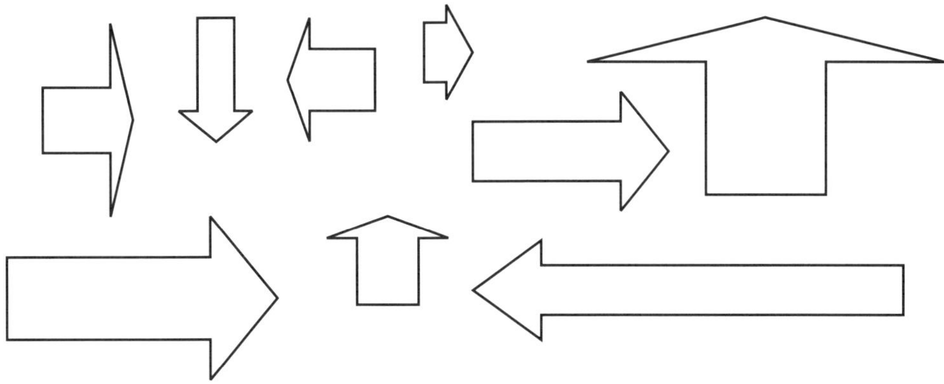

(a) Write C in the two shapes that are congruent.

(b) Write S in two other shapes that are similar.

2  The pentagon below has been divided into triangles.

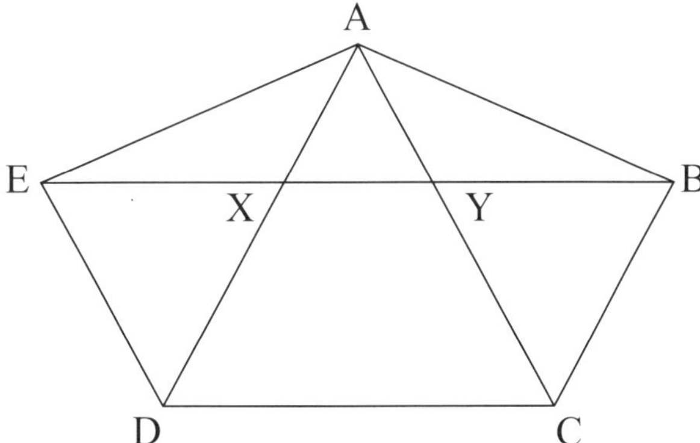

(a) Which triangle in this diagram is congruent to triangle ABY?

....

(b) Which triangle is similar to triangle ACD?

....

Translation

1 

The pattern on the right is made up of different shaped tiles.

Write X inside any shape that is a translation of the marked tile.

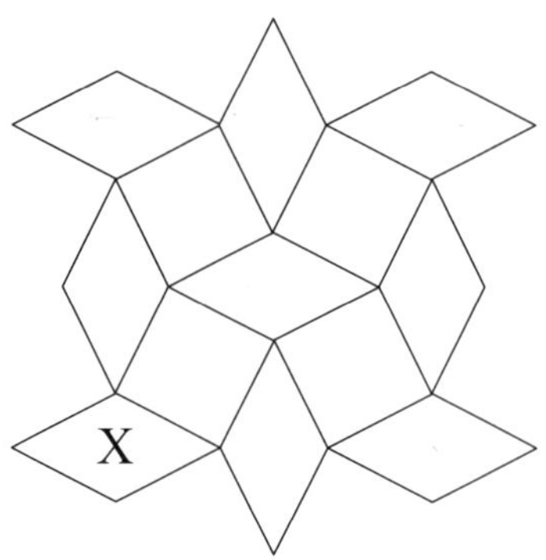

2 

Look at the diagram below.

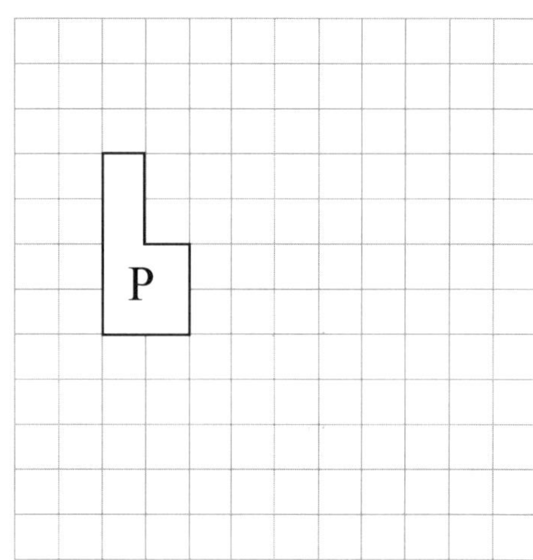

Shape P is translated 3 squares to the right and 2 squares down.

Draw shape P in its new position, and label it P_1.

3 

Triangles A, B and C have been drawn on a grid.

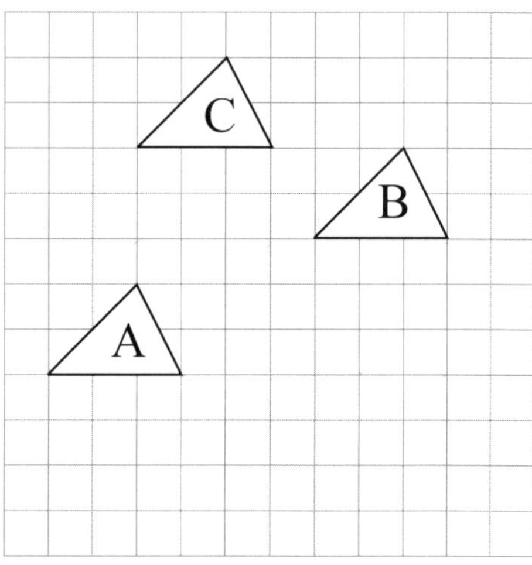

(a) Describe the translation that transforms triangle A to triangle B.

....

(b) Describe the translation that transforms triangle B to triangle C.

....

Enlargement

1  Draw an enlargement of this triangle, with scale factor 3 and centre of enlargement X:

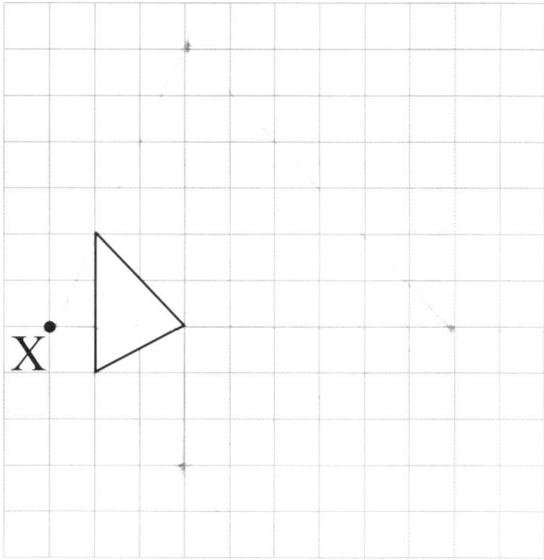

2  Look at the diagram on the right.

(a) What is the scale factor of the enlargement from R to S?

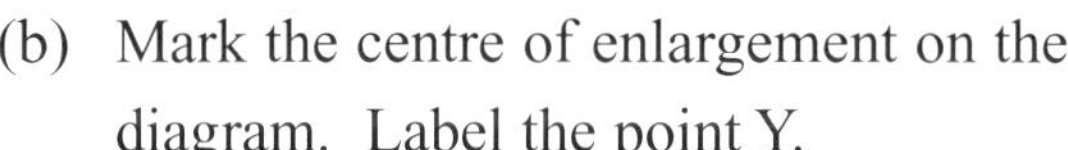

(b) Mark the centre of enlargement on the diagram. Label the point Y.

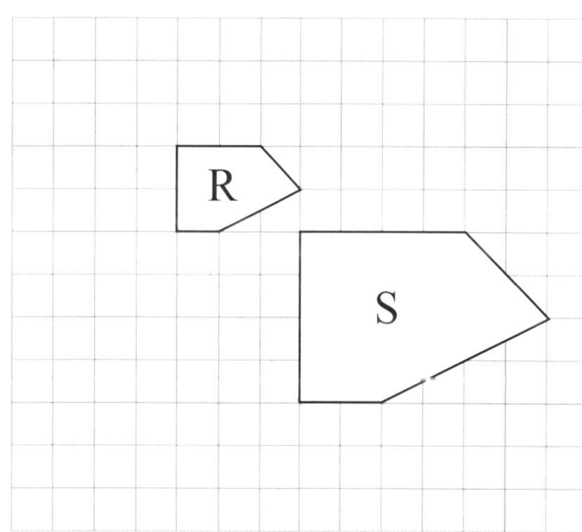

3  Shape W is an enlargement of shape V.

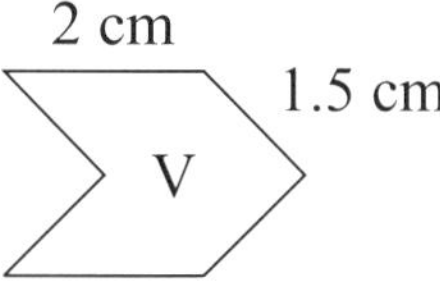

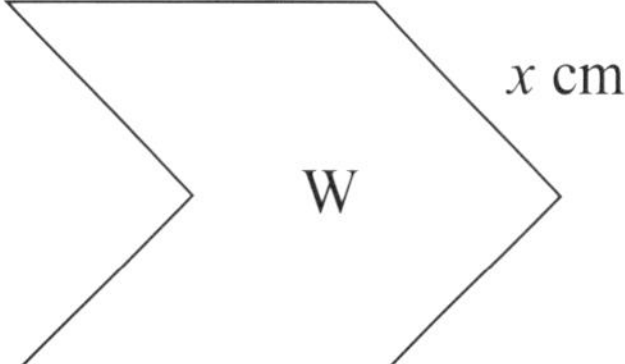

Not to scale

(a) What is the scale factor of the enlargement?

....

(b) Work out the value of x.

....

Rotation

1  Draw the shape below after it has been rotated through 180° about the origin.

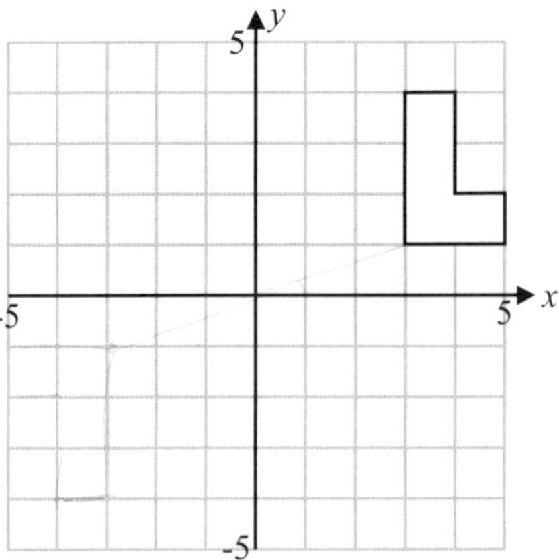

2 Rotate this shape 90° anticlockwise about X.

3 Shape A can be rotated onto shape B and shape C.

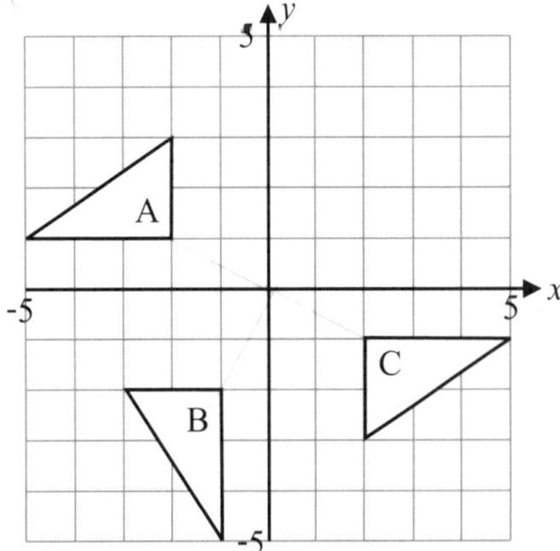

(a) Describe the rotation of shape A to shape B.

....

(b) Describe the rotation of shape A to shape C.

....

Reflection

1  Reflect the triangle in the x-axis:

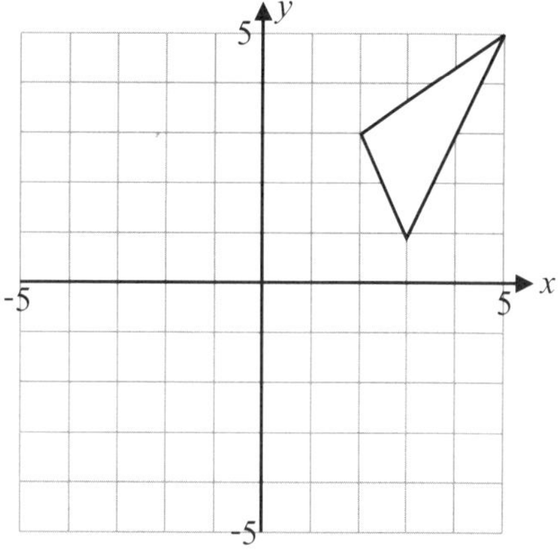

2 Reflect these shapes in the mirror lines shown:

(a)

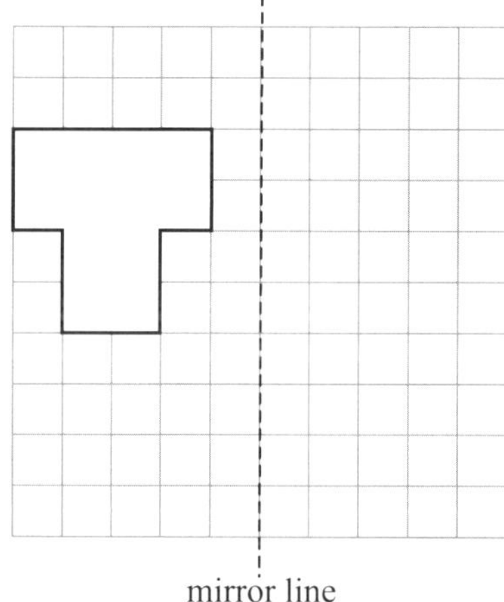

(b)

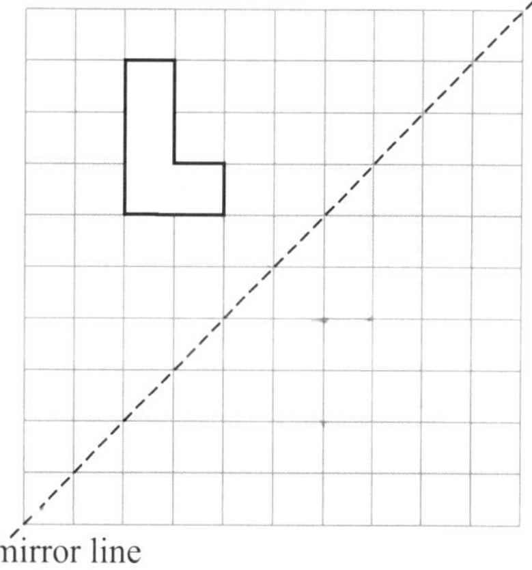

3 Shape B is a reflection of shape A:

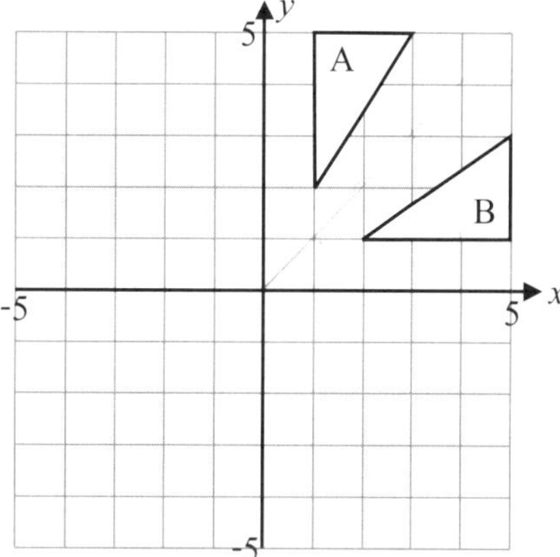

(a) Draw the mirror line for the reflection.

(b) Write down the equation of the mirror line.

....

Angles & Other Bits Mini-Exam (1)

1  Shape A in the diagram can be transformed into shapes B and C.

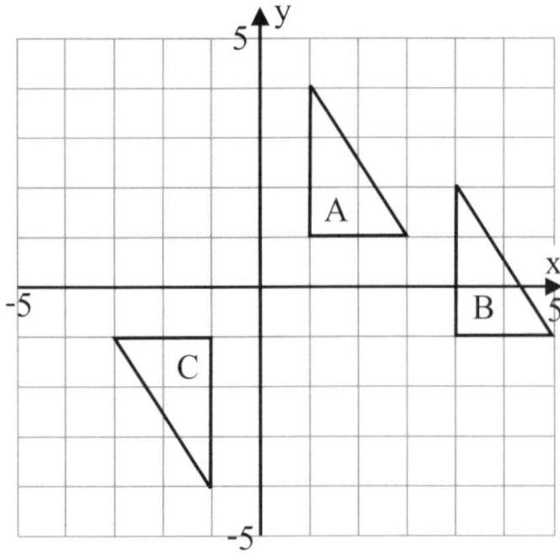

(a) Describe the transformation of shape A to shape B.

....

(b) Describe the transformation of shape A to shape C.

....

(c) Draw the reflection of shape A in the y-axis. Label this shape D.

2  Draw an enlargement of the shape below using a scale factor of 3.
Use the point marked X as the centre of enlargement.

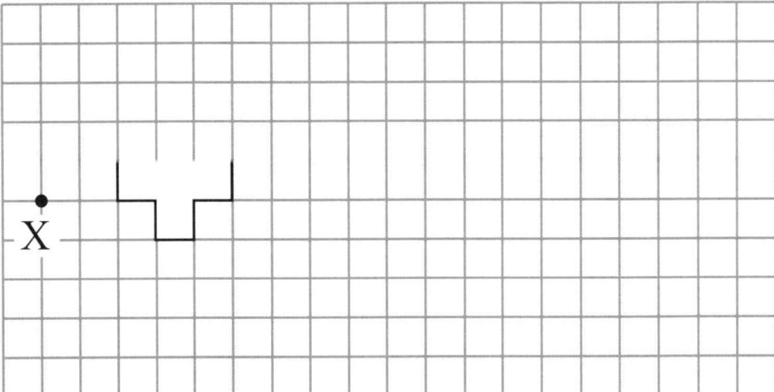

3 Which shapes below are congruent to shape A?

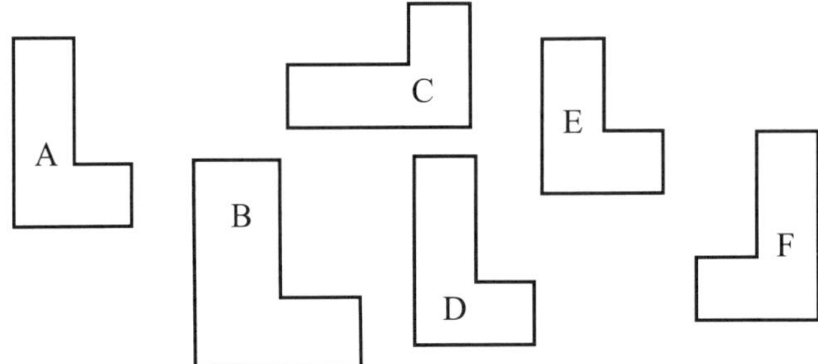

....

Angles & Other Bits Mini-Exam (1)

4  Look at the diagram below.

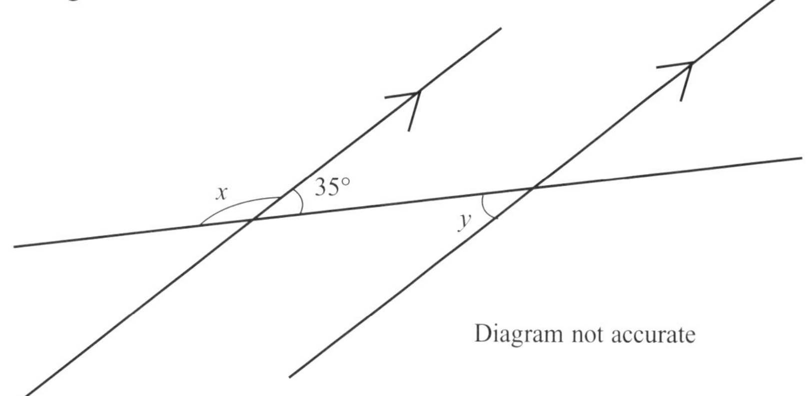

(a) Calculate angle x.

....

(b) Find angle y.

....

(c) Show on the diagram another angle that is the same size as angle x. Label this p.

5  A boat is at the position shown on this map.

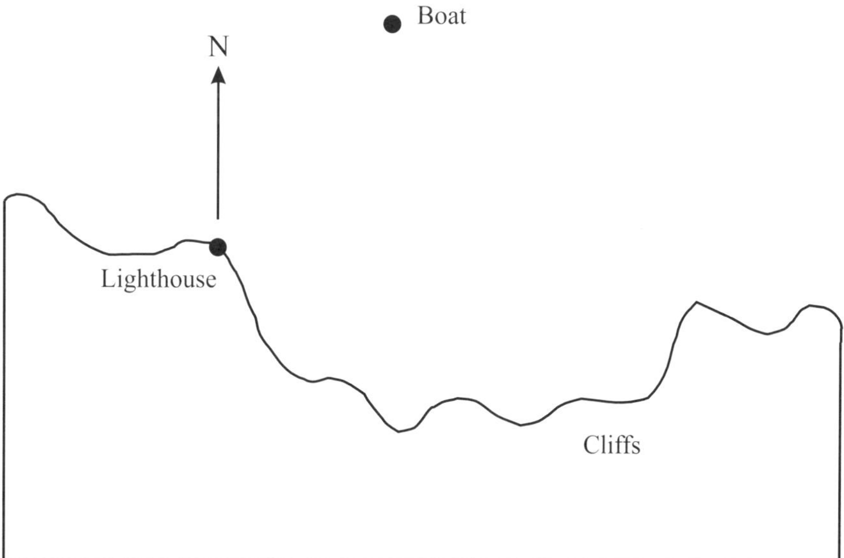

(a) Find the three-figure bearing of the boat from the lighthouse.

....

(b) A seagull is sitting on the cliff. It is on a bearing of 110° from the lighthouse.
Mark the position of the seagull on the diagram with an X.

Angles & Other Bits Mini-Exam (2)

1 A film starts at 9.20 pm and finishes at 11.05 pm.

(a) Write down the start and finish times using the 24-hour clock.

....

(b) How long does the film last?

....

2 The timetable below is for trains travelling from Carlisle to Preston.

Carlisle	1535	1635	1730	1831
Penrith	1553	1653	1618	1849
Oxenholme	1605	1705	1800	1901
Lancaster	1637	1737	1832	1933
Preston	1709	1809	1904	2005

(a) What is the latest you could catch a train in Carlisle if you have to be in Preston by 6.30 pm?

....

(b) How long would the journey take if you were to take this train?

....

3 A bus takes 20 minutes to travel 18 km.

What is the average speed of the bus in kilometres per hour?

....

....

4 The graph shows a cyclist's journey on a day out. She cycles from home to a village, where she stops for a rest. Then she cycles a bit further before stopping for a picnic. After lunch, the cyclist returns home without stopping.

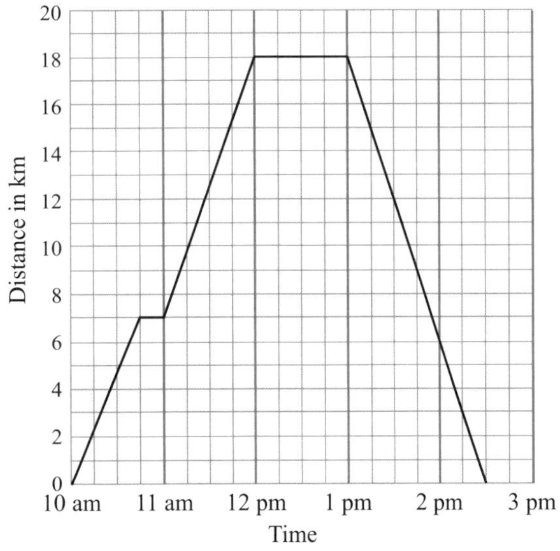

Distance in km: 0, 2, 4, 6, 8, 10, 12, 14, 16, 18, 20
Time: 10 am, 11 am, 12 pm, 1 pm, 2 pm, 3 pm

(a) How far is the village from the cyclist's home?

....

(b) How long did she rest in the village?

....

(c) What was her speed for the journey home?

....

Angles & Other Bits Mini-Exam (2)

5  ABC is a triangle with AC = BC.

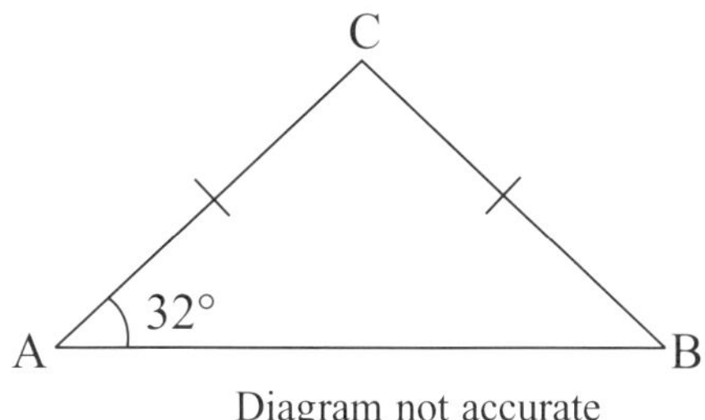

Diagram not accurate

(a) What type of triangle is ABC?

....

(b) Calculate angle ACB.

....

....

6  In the diagram below, DE and FG are parallel.

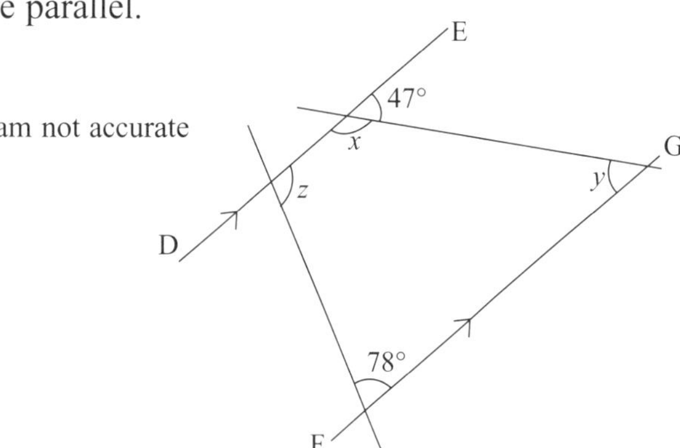

Diagram not accurate

Calculate the size of:

(a) angle x

....

(b) angle y

....

(c) angle z

....

7 In the diagram, PQ is a straight line.
Calculate the value of x.

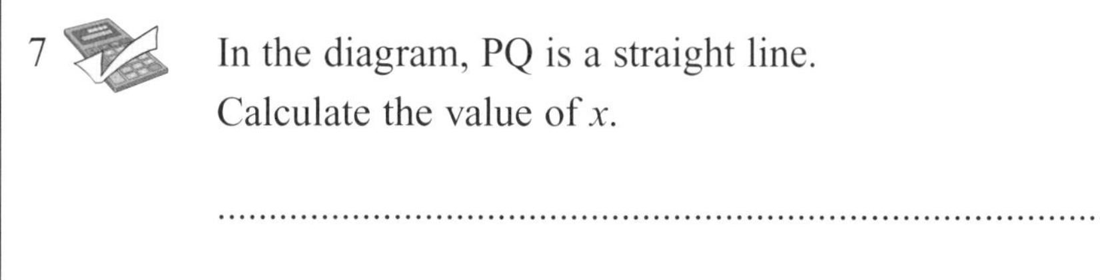

....

....

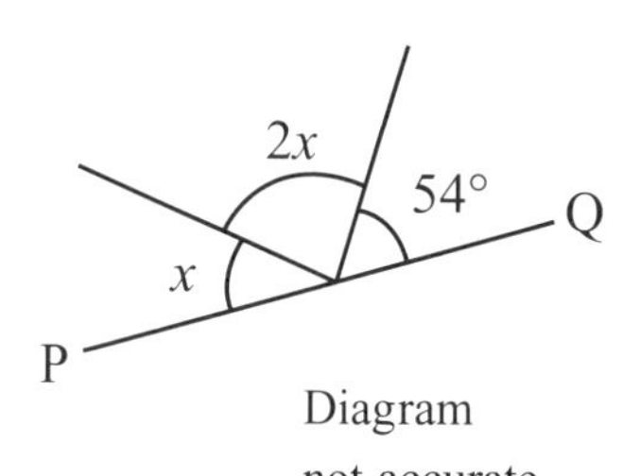

Diagram not accurate

8 A map is drawn with a scale of 1 cm to 2 miles.

(a) Two towns are 39 miles apart. How far apart are they on the map?

....

(b) How long is a river which on the map is 3.5 cm long?

....

Powers

1 Work out the value of:

(a) 7^3 ....

....

(b) 1^5 ....

2 Which is bigger, 2^5 or 6^2? Show your working.

....

....

3 If $3^x = 81$, find the value of x.

....

....

4 What is the value of 5 cubed take away 10 squared?

....

....

5 Work out $3^2 \times 4^3 \times 6^1$.

....

....

....

6 Work out the value of $2.6^2 + 4^3$.

....

....

Square Roots

1 What is the square root of 81?

2 Use the fact that $5^2 = 25$ and $6^2 = 36$ to estimate the value of $\sqrt{30}$.

3 Find the value of $3^2 + \sqrt{0.16}$.

4 This square has an area of 121 cm^2.

How long are the sides of the square?

Area = 121 cm^2

5 Find the value of $\dfrac{1}{(0.25)^2}$.

Number Patterns and Sequences

1 Write down the next number in these number patterns:

(a) 7, 11, 15, 19, ...

(b) 3, 6, 12, 24, ...

2 Fill in the missing numbers in these number patterns:

(a) .... , 17, 14, 11, ... , 5

(b) 480, ... , 120, 60, ... , 15

3  Fill in the next two numbers in this sequence.

13, 10, 7, 4, ... , ...

4  Look at the rows of numbers below:

Row 1: $1 = 1$
Row 2: $1 + 3 = 4$
Row 3: $1 + 3 + 5 = 9$
Row 4: $1 + 3 + 5 + 7 = 16$

(a) Write down Row 5.

....

(b) The row totals are 1, 4, 9, 16, …

What is the special name for these numbers?

....

5  A number sequence begins: 7, 12, 17, 22, 27, …

(a) Write down the next two numbers in this sequence.

.... and ....

(b) Will the number 97 be in this sequence? Explain your answer.

....

....

Number Patterns and Sequences

1 Here is a number sequence with two terms missing: 7, 13, 19, ?, 31, ?, ...

(a) Write down the two missing numbers in the sequence.

.... and ....

(b) Explain the pattern for finding the next number in the sequence.

....

....

2 The *n*th term of a sequence is given by $u_n = 2n + 3$.

(a) What are the first three terms of the sequence?

u_1 = ... u_2 = ... u_3 = ...

(b) What is the 10th term of this sequence?

....

3 The first 3 terms of a sequence are: 2, 4, 6, …

(a) Faye says the next number is 8. Explain Faye's rule.

....

....

(b) Sohid says you add the previous two numbers together to get the next term,
for example: 2 + 4 = 6

What will be the next two numbers in Sohid's sequence?

.... and ....

4 Find an expression for the *n*th term of this sequence: 1, 6, 11, 16, …

....

....

Negative Numbers

1  The temperature in a meat freezer was –18 °C. Unfortunately the freezer broke down.
The temperature inside the freezer rose by 6 °C while it was being repaired.
What was the new temperature inside the freezer?

....

2  Calculate:

(a) $4 - 10 + -3$

....

(b) $-4 - (2 \times -3)$

....

3  Look at the equations below and fill in the missing information.

(a) Fill in the missing numbers:

(i) $-3 + \square = +2$

(ii) $\square \times -4 = -12$

(b) Fill in the missing signs (+ or –):

(i) $-2 + \square\, 6 = -8$

(ii) $\square\, 24 \div -3 = +8$

4  Solve these problems:

(a) A shipwreck lies 248 m under the sea. A diver has gone down 189 m.
How much further does she need to go to get to the wreck?

....

(b) A club running a disco made a loss of £975, which made their bank balance –£975.
The club then received a donation of £450.

What is the club's bank balance now?

....

Basic Algebra

1  Look at the two rods and answer the questions.

(a) What is the length of this rod? Simplify your answer.

$5p$ $3p$

....

(b) What is the length of the piece of rod marked x?

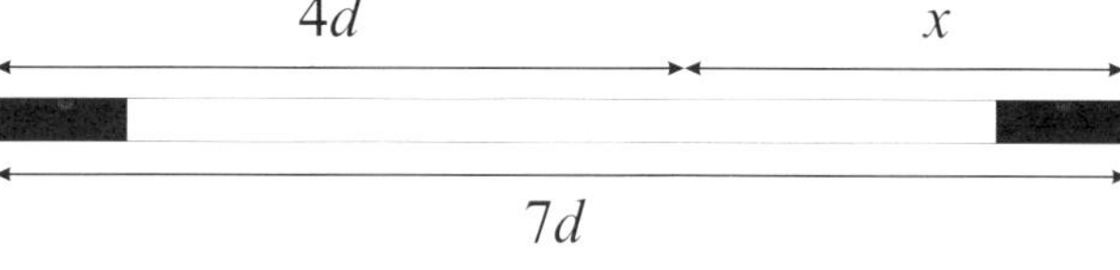

....

2  Simplify the following:

(a) $r + r + r$ ....

(b) $3n + 7n$ ....

(c) $4a + 5b - a + 2b$ ....

3  Tick the correct expression for the perimeter of each shape:

(a)

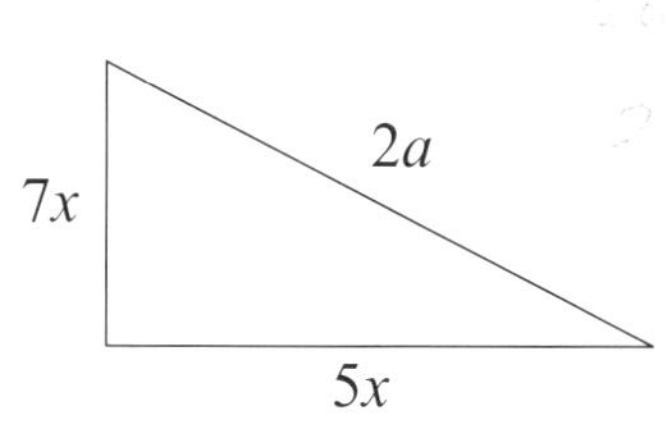

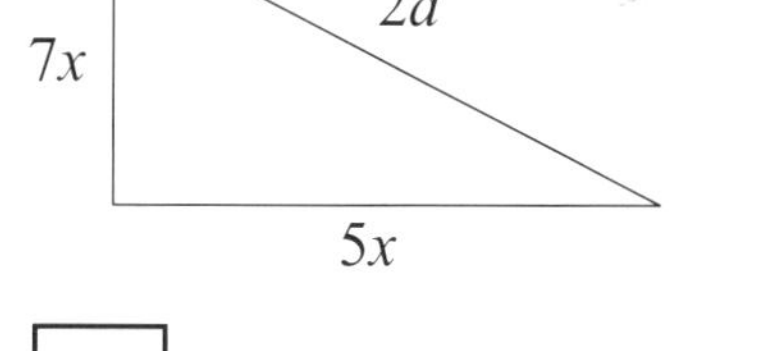

☐ $14ax$

☐ $12x + 2a$

☐ $\frac{35x^2}{2}$

(b)

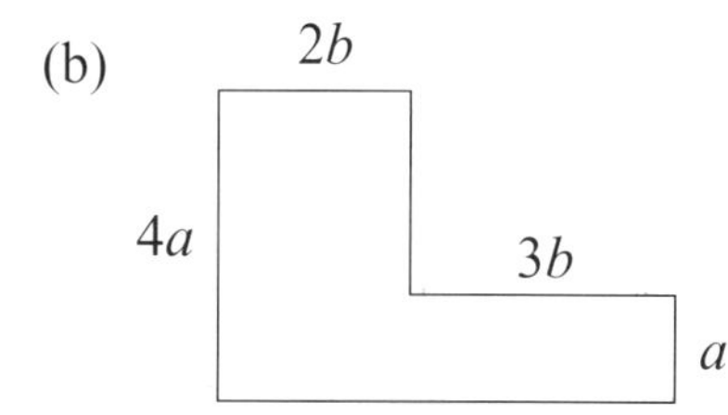

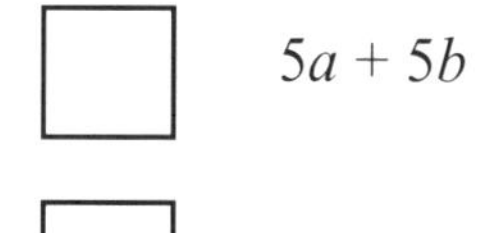

☐ $5a + 5b$

☐ $24a^2b^2$

☐ $8a + 10b$

Basic Algebra

1  Multiply out these brackets:

(a) $4(p-2)$

....

(b) $7(2m+3n-q)$

....

2 Multiply out these brackets and then simplify:

(a) $4(s+2t)+2(3s-t)$

....

(b) $5(3d-e)-4e$

....

3  Write the number of the formula from the box that matches each statement below:

① $2x-7$	② $\frac{5x-7}{2}$	③ $x-14$
④ $\frac{5(x-7)}{2}$	⑤ $2(x-7)$	⑥ $5x-\frac{7}{2}$

(a) I think of a number. I subtract 7, and then I double the result. ....

(b) I think of a number and then multiply it by 5. I subtract 7 and then halve the result. ....

4  Charley thinks the perimeter of the rectangle below is $P = 2L + 2W$.
Lucy says it is $P = 2(L + W)$.

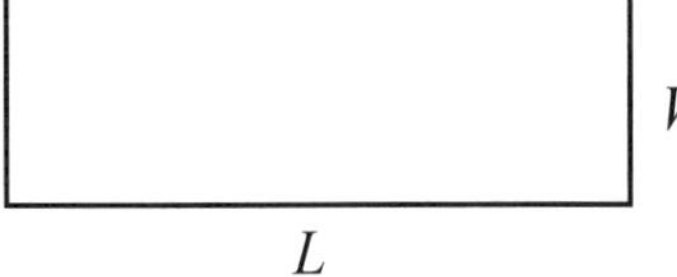

Who is right? Explain your answer.

....

....

....

Making Formulas from Words

1 To convert kilometres into miles, Tasmin said that you divide the number of kilometres by 8 and multiply the answer by 5.

(a) Write this rule as a formula, using k to represent the number of kilometres and m to represent the number of miles.

(b) Use your formula to convert 110 kilometres into miles.

2 Write down the formulas asked for below.

(a) Write a formula for y in terms of x if the value of y is found by multiplying x by 3 and subtracting 10.

(b) Write a formula for p in terms of n if the value of p is found by squaring n and dividing the result by 2.

3 To hire a cement mixer Alex pays £50 per day plus a deposit of £300.

(a) How much would Alex have to pay to hire the cement mixer for 3 days?

(b) Write a formula to show the total cost (£C) of hiring the cement mixer for d days.

Trial and Improvement

1  Solve the equations below:

(a) $4x = 28$

(b) $7x - 2 = 33$

2 Solve the following equation for n:

$$4n + 3 = 2n - 7$$

3  Use trial and improvement to find the value of x to one decimal place where $x^3 + 7 = 42$.

4 The shaded area on the right can be found using the formula below:

Area = $2x^2 + x$

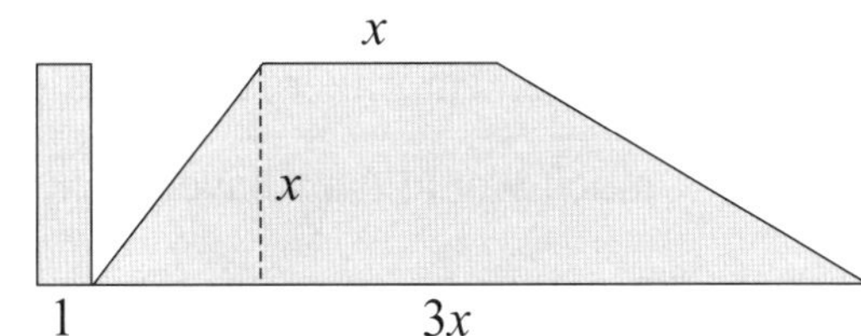

The area of this shape is 63 cm^2.

Using trial and improvement, find the height of the shape correct to one decimal place.

Algebra Mini-Exam (1)

1 This question is about negative numbers.

(a) Arrange these numbers in order, from lowest to highest:

–2, 3, 7, 0, –12, 10

....

(b) What is the difference between –13 and 12?

....

2  The approximate rule for converting inches into centimetres is:

$$i = \frac{2c}{5},$$

where i represents the number of inches, and c represents the number of centimetres.

(a) Convert 15 centimetres into inches.

....

(b) Is the statement in the box below true or false? Circle the word TRUE or FALSE.

100 cm ≈ 250 inches

TRUE **FALSE**

3  Simplify the following:

(a) $m + 3m - 2m$ ....

(b) $7r - 2p - 4r + 6p$ ....

4 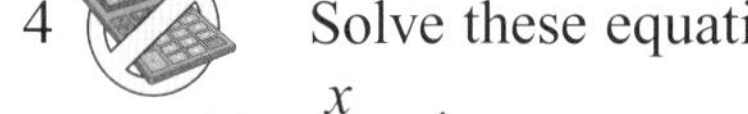 Solve these equations for x:

(a) $\frac{x}{5} = 4$ ....

(b) $7x - 4 = 2x + 1$ ....

5 Calculate:

(a) 2^5 ....

(b) $\sqrt{100}$ ....

(c) x^3, if $x = 3$ ....

Algebra Mini-Exam (1)

6 Warner's Garage sells cans of coke for 65p each.

(a) Write a formula for the total cost, C pence, of buying n cans of coke.

....

(b) The total cost of buying n cans of coke is £T. Write a formula for T in terms of n.

....

7 Answer these questions about a particular sequence:

(a) Fill in the gaps in this sequence:

5, 8, 11, ☐, ☐, 20

(b) Write an expression for the nth term of this sequence.

....

8 Solve these equations for x:

(a) $x^2 = 144$ ....

(b) $3x^2 = 75$ ....

9 Answer the questions that follow.

(a) Multiply out this expression:

$3(2x + 1) =$ ....

(b) Hence or otherwise, solve this equation:

$3(2x + 1) = 33$

....

10 Len and Sam are talking.

(a) Len has m pence more than Sam. If Sam has v pence, write an expression to show how much Len has.

....

(b) Len has a collection of books. Each book is g cm thick.
Write an expression to show how many of Len's books will fit on a shelf s cm long.

....

Algebra Mini-Exam (2)

1 This square has an area of 484 cm². Find x.

....

....

....

2 Look at the number line below.

(a) Mark an X on the number line at –25.

(b) What is the difference between –25 and +48?

....

3 Algebra is a kind of mathematical shorthand.

(a) Write expressions to match these statements. The first one has already been done.

(i) multiply q by 7 and add 3 .... $7q + 3$

(ii) double p and subtract r ....

(iii) divide the sum of 7 and n by x ....

(b) If $c = -2$ and $d = -3.5$, find the value of:

(i) $\frac{10.75 + c}{d}$ ....

(ii) cd ....

4 Find an expression for the nth term of this sequence:

2, 7, 12, 17, …

....

5 If $x^3 + 3 = 42$, use trial and improvement to find the value of x to one decimal place.

....

....

....

....

Algebra Mini-Exam (2)

6  The quantities l, m and k are connected by the following formula:

$$m = \sqrt{\frac{k}{l}}$$

Find m, correct to one decimal place, when $k = 42$ and $l = 6.4$.

....

7 Evaluate:

(a) -30×-6 ....

(b) 9^3 ....

(c) $\sqrt{289}$ ....

8 If $a = 7$ and $b = -14$, calculate:

(a) $2a + b$ ....

(b) $\frac{a}{b}$ ....

(c) $3ab$ ....

(d) b^2 ....

9 Write down the first three numbers in these sequences:

(a) Square numbers: .... , ... , ...

(b) Start with 7 and multiply the previous term by 3: .... , ... , ...

10 The volume of this solid can be found using the formula $V = 6x^2$.

Calculate the volume of the solid when $x = 4.5$ cm.

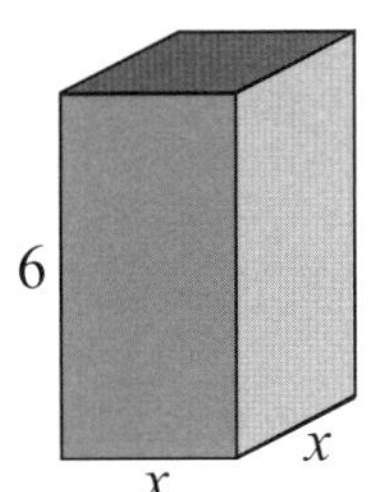

....

....

....